Prequel to The Dome Chronicles

One Damn Thing

After Another

Garry Leeson

One Damn Thing After Another
© 2024 Garry Leeson

Cover design: Rebekah Wetmore, from a photo in the author's collection
Editor: Andrew Wetmore

ISBN: 978-1-998149-41-4
First edition November, 2024

Moose House Publications
2475 Perotte Road
Annapolis County, NS B0S 1A0
moosehousepress.com
info@moosehousepress.com

Moose House Publications recognizes the support of the Province of Nova Scotia. We are pleased to work in partnership with the Department of Communities, Culture and Heritage to develop and promote our cultural resources for all Nova Scotians.

We live and work in Mi'kma'ki, the ancestral and unceded territory of the Mi'kmaw people. This territory is covered by the "Treaties of Peace and Friendship" which Mi'kmaw and Wolastoqiyik (Maliseet) people first signed with the British Crown in 1725. The treaties did not deal with surrender of lands and resources but in fact recognized Mi'kmaq and Wolastoqiyik (Maliseet) title and established the rules for what was to be an ongoing relationship between nations. We are all Treaty people.

Also by Garry Leeson

The Dome Chronicles

The Secret of the Spring*

Dan Johnson's Ashes*

Less than Innocent (co-author)*

*available from Moose House Publications
moosehousepress.com

For Brenden, Timothy, Zoe, Emily and, as always, Andrea.

Disclaimer

These stories shine an enhanced light on past days. They are stories, not court reporting, so there may be some divergence between the events as told and what other participants may remember, and some names have been changed

One Damn Thing After Another

One Damn Thing After Another

Garry Leeson

Constable Leeson

1: What the hell have I done?

Glancing into the mirror on the morning of my first day as a police cadet in 1963, I was startled by the stranger in the blue serge uniform leering back at me.

I hadn't intended to join the police force. I'd just thought that a fake enlistment attempt would provide an amusing story to share with my buddies. But this was taking a joke too damned far.

The day before I had received a phone call directing me to report to the Don Mills Police Station and I dreaded going but couldn't call in sick on my first day. There was no getting out of it...I had to face the music.

~

All this nonsense had started two months earlier.

It was that darned sign posted high on the side of Metro Toronto Police Headquarters, a huge poster depicting a stern-looking policeman with the caption, "Do you stand out?" He seemed to be pointing his finger directly at me.

It was lunch hour, and the streets were crowded with businessmen in suits looking very clean and important. I, on the other hand, was unshaven and wearing my favourite faded jeans and plaid shirt. As I looked around me I realized that I definitely did stand out.

That's when I got the crazy idea. I'd go in and pretend that I was going to join the police force. It would be a real hoot and my buddy, Ron, and the rest of the guys would love it.

After gathering up the courage to enter the iconic old building to pursue my prank, I was ushered into a small office where a large, intimidating officer in full dress uniform pointed to a chair in front of his desk. Noticing his Sam Browne belt and holster shined to perfection, I discreetly rubbed the toes of my dirty cowboy boots against my pant legs.

"Why do you want to be a policeman?" No word of introduction, just a cursory sizing-up and the bark.

Leaning forward and placing my elbow on his desk, I rested my chin on my clenched fist, giving him my best impression of "The Thinker." Looking straight into his eyes, I said, "I've always wanted to be a police-man"

I couldn't believe it. The guy actually believed me. He had absolutely no sense of humour.

He gave me a warm smile and, switching into the "I'm your buddy" routine, the huge cop confided in me. "Look, Garry, you barely meet the height requirements, and at—what?—138 pounds, you would hardly be much of a visual deterrent to crime. But if that's horse manure I smell on those boots and you know your way around a horse, we might find a spot for you on the Mounted Unit. If you clean up for your next interview, I'll process your application and see what I can do."

I skipped down the steps onto King Street laughing to myself. I could hardly wait to tell the boys.

When I finally met them later that week, I told them about my funny adventure, but they didn't react at all the way I thought they would. They seemed to think I was a traitor for even go-ing into Police Headquarters, let alone almost signing up as a cop. Some even hinted at my subcon-sciously *wanting* to join up.

Ron Bond came down on me the hardest, saying that if I ever became a cop, that would be the end of our friendship.

When I insisted, "It was just a joke," it didn't stop him from go-ing on and on about how despic-able an act it would be. I just fin-ished my beer and left. "Who needs them, anyway?"

Ron Bond

I was heading out west to visit my sister, Isabel, and her family for a month. It was going to be a fun trip; my brother-in-law, Colin, had a young horse he wanted to break, and I was looking forward to giving him

In Saskatchewan when I was supposed to be at the recruiting office

a hand.

Six weeks later, when I got back, I decided to call Ron and clear the air about my police interview.

There was no answer when I rang his doorbell, but as I turned to go, I saw his car coming down the street. He parked but didn't get out right away.

I thought he was still angry with me, but when he did get out, I saw why he had hesitated. He was dressed in a police uniform!

I couldn't believe my eyes. After all, he had accused me of, he sure had a lot of explaining to do.

After a few hours and several beers, Ron's reasons for changing his mind about the police force started to make sense. And then he had the gall to start on me! *Misery loves company*, I thought.

He was relentless.., sounding more enthusiastic and convincing than the recruiting officer had. But he probably was wasting his time badgering me because, as I explained, a letter had come from Police Head-quarters asking me to report for further processing while I was away, and I had ignored it.

I had probably blown my chances.

But then again, at nineteen years old I was already married and out of work. A couple of tedious months of doing whatever policemen do, supported by a regular pay-check, wouldn't hurt while I decided what I really wanted to do with my life, so I thought I'd give it another try.

The next day, sporting a new haircut, my best suit and whatever courage I could muster, I returned to Police Headquarters and searched out the recruiting officer.

"What are you doing here?" he demanded.

"Well, sir," I lied, "I was hoping I might hear from you after our first interview and it's been quite a while, so I was wondering why I wasn't being considered. I even gained five pounds for you, and I've been working out, too."

"Mr. Leeson, I do indeed remember your file. We sent you a letter for follow-up meetings and you didn't even have the courtesy of replying to us."

Conjuring up my best shocked look, perfected in my high school years, I said, "I never got it. I waited and waited, but I figured I hadn't made the mark."

Trying to look dejected, I got up, head down, and turned to leave.

Before I made it to the door, he stopped me. "Hang on a minute," he said. "I can't understand how you didn't get a registered letter, but you seem sincere, so come with me."

Yes! He'd bought it.

He stayed with me while I was weighed. Right on 143, a testament to my honesty! He still had my original file, complete with background check, so he hustled me right down the hall to the Police Surgeon for a complete physical.

After all the probing, tapping and a request to breathe in and breathe out and cough, the old doctor put aside his stethoscope and asked me to bend my arm and make a muscle. I gave the best I could and, after he finished giving each bicep a gentle squeeze, he laughingly recited a line of poetry I have never forgotten: "The muscles on his spindly arms stood out like sparrows' ankles."

Anyway, despite that pathetic first impression, he gave me a passing grade and I was in.

I spent another embarrassing hour in a musty basement room, where an aging constable and his assistant tried to outfit me with a uniform. There were long racks of tunics, trousers and shirts, but everything they pulled out swam on me. At one point the men had a great laugh at my expense when the only jacket that seemed the perfect size turned out to be a policewoman's.

They finally found a complete kit close enough in size to do me until I could be measured and properly fitted for a new one. I headed home with all my gear in two shopping bags to await my first assignment.

When that assignment finally came, I double-checked myself in the long mirror and headed out. I walked down our long driveway to the main road decked out in the second-hand uniform my mother had altered for me, feeling self-conscious and ridiculous. I had borrowed my dad's old black lunch box...I remembered seeing policemen carrying similar ones on their way to work.

It was only a short walk to the nearest bus stop, but I had only gone a few yards in that direction when a car pulled over and a dignified older man opened his door, stepped out and, looking directly at me, said, "Can I give you a lift, Officer?"

I looked over my shoulder to see who was standing behind me. *My god, he's talking to me!*

I climbed in beside him, remembering all the times I had tried unsuccessfully to hitch rides on this same stretch of road when I was still a lowly teenage civilian.

As we drove along, he chatted away about how much he admired the police force and what a wonderful job it had been doing over the years.

I thanked him and in my most humble voice said, "Well, sir, we're just doing our job."

He replied that I was being too modest.

Jesus, if he'd only known.

He dropped me off at an intersection where several people were waiting for a bus.

Not sure of exactly where I was, and forgetting I was in uniform, I approached the lineup and asked a man reading a newspaper, "Excuse me, sir, could you tell me where the police station is?"

He gave me the strangest look and, after a long pause and without saying a word, pointed with his paper toward 33 Division, clearly visible less than a block away.

What's with this guy? I wondered.

Then I caught sight of myself in the bus shelter window and quickly said, "Well done, sir, you'd be surprised how many people don't know that."

I headed off in the direction of the police station thinking, *This being a policeman isn't half bad. I could get used to this!*

2: Here's looking at you, Sergeant Saul

My first three weeks as a police cadet were spent, for the most part, not wiping out crime as I had expected, but wiping out police cars, and washing them and filling them with gas. I swabbed out the drunk tank each morning and, generally, ran errands for the real policemen.

Although my new tailor-made uniform had arrived and I was wearing it to and from work each day, mostly it hung in my locker while I sported a pair of blue coveralls more suited to my assignments.

Finally, I received orders to report to the Police College, and I looked forward to the end of my drudgery and to some leisure time in the classroom. In those days Metropolitan Toronto had its own training centre in a converted two-story former elementary school in Willowdale, in the north end of the city.

Me and Sgt. Saul

The schoolyard had been paved and was used as a parade ground. I hadn't thought much about drilling and marching. I knew that there was probably going to be a certain amount of it, but after all, this was not the army; it was the police force. My marching skills were sadly lacking.

In the 1960s all Canadian high schools still had a mandatory Cadet Program which all students were obliged to take part in. The only exemptions permitted were to band members.

I quickly signed up to play the trumpet and ended up sitting in the shade playing Colonel Bogie while my classmates, sweating in their wool khaki uniforms, marched up and down the schoolyard.

I wondered if I might come up with something similar now.

We all gathered in a large classroom that first morning. A clean-cut young policeman told us to take a seat anywhere we liked.

Ah, this the life, I thought as I settled myself down in a seat at the back of the room and busied myself opening my notebook and selecting pens and pencils. I had just removed my tie and was leaning back in my chair when the room was rocked with a throaty bellow. "Attention!" The word seemed to reverberate and hang in the air.

A tall, straight, stern-looking policeman in a gleaming uniform was shouting at us. He looked to be about fifty years old and his presence oozed authority.

We all jumped to our feet and gave our individual interpretations of what "Attention" should look like.

Addressing us as stupid bastards, he, in a gruff voice, described the proper way to stand to attention. Then he introduced himself as Sergeant Saul and informed us that he was to be our Drill Instructor and general disciplinarian. He went on to say that he had observed us arriving that morning and without a doubt we were the sorriest bunch of dirty buggers he had ever laid eyes on.

"All that is going to change," he shouted. "Now get your lazy asses down to that parade ground!"

And so the marching began, day after day of "By the left, quick march, I said LEFT, you stupid bastards", or "Into line, left turn. Does that look like a line, you nitwits?"

After what seemed like an eternity of abuse, all but one member of our class seemed to be getting the hang of it. Poor Cadet Lumsden was still stumbling, turning the wrong way and constantly skipping along trying to get back in step, and no amount of swearing and cajoling on Sergeant Saul's part made his performance improve.

Eagan was a big, healthy farm boy from northern Ontario who, at first glance, looked the sort who would make a good policeman. However, there was definitely something missing in the brains department. As some of the less sensitive cadets put it, "He's a few bricks shy of a load," you know, "A few pickles short of a jar," or, "All of his rooms weren't plastered."

I knew it was all over for Lumsden one morning when we paraded for duty. He had forgotten his memo book and Sergeant Saul was busy cutting him a new arse hole, as he liked to put it. When he finished his tirade, he lowered his voice and, almost pleading, said, "Listen, Lumsden: if you're going to make it, you're really have to pull up your socks."

To our astonishment, Lumsden actually squatted down and pulled up his socks. The next day he was transferred to the city's Parking Meter Control Unit.

I would often see him in later years. He seemed very happy, sporting his brown uniform and tooling around on his Pie Wagon, as the three-wheeled motorcycles were called.

The marching and drilling were not easy for me, but my real problem was passing muster when Sgt. Saul did his inspections each morning. Try as I might, I couldn't seem to please him. I spent hours every night working on my kit, ironing, polishing and brushing, and still he would always find something wrong and bring it to my attention in his not-so-subtle manner.

If he found a single hair on my blue serge uniform, he would exclaim for all to hear, "Did you have much trouble getting the dog off your uniform this morning, Leeson?" If my tie was not hanging perfectly perpendicular, he would straighten it saying, "Mummy dressed us a little funny this morning didn't she?"

If he couldn't find anything else to complain about he would say, "Get a haircut!" which I frequently did but it never seemed to be enough, I was starting to look like Yul Brynner.

The night before our final day on the cadet course, I made up my mind that my turnout was going to be impeccable. I vowed that I would be the cleanest, shiniest son of a bitch on that parade ground. I pulled out all the stops. I spent hours using cotton swabs dipped in ice water to put a high shine on my boots and Sam Browne belt. My uniform was cleaned and pressed to perfection; there wasn't a crease, smudge or a hair to be found anywhere. I also vacuumed my car seats so that my uniform wouldn't pick up any debris as I drove to the college in the morning.

I went to bed with what hair I had left perfectly coiffed and held in place with a nylon stocking. I was ready. There was nothing, nothing that Saul would be able to find fault with.

I stayed up so late that night that I slightly overslept the next morning, but I knew that, if I hurried, I would still be in good time for the inspection parade. I dressed carefully avoiding contact with anything that might tarnish my perfect appearance. I skipped breakfast; I didn't want to sit too long it might spoil the crease in my pants.

I was cautiously making my way to my car when I heard a terrible scream, it sounded almost like a human baby in pain.

On the other side of the car, there on the ground was a stray cat with a half-eaten baby rabbit in his mouth. The cat dropped the little creature and disappeared into the tall grass. The tiny rabbit lay whimpering and unable to move.

He was so badly mangled I knew he was beyond help. The only humane thing to do was to put him out of his misery as soon as possible.

Gritting my teeth and wincing, I stepped forward and brought my heavy boot down as hard as could on the poor bunny's head. Death was instantaneous and his suffering was over.

With a heavy heart, but comforted by the notion that I had done the right thing, I jumped into my car and headed for the Police College.

By the time I arrived, the rest of the cadets had already begun to assemble on the parade ground. I hurried over and joined them.

We formed up in three lines of open order and stood rigidly at attention as Sgt. Saul quick-marched over to us with his swagger stick tucked under his arm. He proceeded to weave his way up and down the ranks, making rude comments to certain of my classmates.

I held my breath as he made his way along the front of the row I was standing in. He paused for a moment in front of me and, after looking me over carefully, gave me a reluctant nod of approval.

I was feeling pretty smug and self-satisfied as he swung around to inspect our backs. All my hard work had paid off. I was already beginning to work on my acceptance speech for the best turned-out cadet when I heard the rhythmic click of the Sergeant's heel clips stop directly behind me.

He was gasping and seemed short of breath, but finally blurted out, "What the hell is that?"

He prodded me in the ass with his swagger stick and I looked over my shoulder and down to the back of my trouser leg. There, looking directly at Sergeant Saul, was a tiny eyeball suspended on a long, trailing ribbon of red tissue.

Sgt. Saul and two of the brighter members.

3: On being a cadet

The status of a cadet is a strange one. Unless you look very closely at his uniform and notice the absence of a gun holster and handcuff pouch, you would probably think you were looking at a full-fledged policeman. Although he might be as young as eighteen, a cadet had most of the responsibilities of official constables. He couldn't make arrests for minor offences, but for the more serious indictable offences he, like anyone else, could make a 'Citizens Arrest'.

In my training days, the uniform the cadet wore, in anticipation of his progression to full police constable, had all the compartments for the weapons of the trade. The pants had a long rear pocket for a nightstick and the winter pea jacket had a leather holster in the right pocket.

Although it was strictly *verboten,* the temptation to fill these cavities with weapons of our own was tempting, particularly if we were working the night shift in dangerous parts of the city An older cop gave me a spare nightstick, and I still have the .22-calibre pistol I discreetly carried. I never had to use it, but it was a real source of comfort in tricky situations.

Shortly after attending Police College for the cadet course, I was sent to the traffic division for motorcycle training. It was wonderful experience, just like summer camp.

A group of about twelve of us spent a couple of weeks weaving Harley Davidsons, BMWs, Matchlesses and Indians between pylons on the exhibition parking lot and going for long rides along the lakeshore and through the streets of the west end of the city. It was late fall and I remember the joy I felt as I sent my sidecar careening through the piles of dead leaves that were accumulating at the sides of the roads, sending them flying into the air and on to the windscreens of the bikes behind me.

It was all new to me, and the experience was the closest I have ever come to the thrill I feel when galloping a horse.

Before we finished our training, the weather turned really cold and we were ordered into winter uniforms, which consisted of heavy twill breeches over long wool underwear, with the leather boots and leggings we normally wore covered with tall, insulated galoshes. On top we wore our winter- issue box-neck tunic over the heaviest flannel shirt we could find. We covered all of this with a knee-length black leather coat with a thick sheepskin lining. A long thick scarf and a white helmet with cold-weather flaps completed the ensemble.

It practically doubled my weight and I thought I might need a derrick to get me onto my bike.

My infatuation with the motorcycle was short-lived. By the time I re-turned to my station in Don Mills, winter had set in with a vengeance and the streets were snow-covered and icy. I thought that the motorcycles would be put away for the winter, but instead they were all fitted with sidecars and it was business as usual.

I found out just how impractical this was when I went out on my first patrol. Approaching a corner with a red light, I casually applied the brakes in the way I had been instructed, and found myself sliding out of control all the way through the intersection, with cars skidding to a halt to avoid hitting me, the drivers honking their horns and shouting very disrespectful things.

After that experience, I realized that there was a knack to riding motorcycles in the winter. First, you had to plan ahead. If you wanted to stop at any particular spot you had to start applying the brakes gradually about one city block in advance. It was touch and go making a turn, as the bike didn't necessarily go in the direction that you turned the handlebars. It was often necessary to, simply, go where you were taken and, if anybody was watching, act as if you intended to be there, which was not that convincing when you ended up in a snowbank.

Only the police department would be allowed to operate a vehicle as dangerous as the bike was in winter. I was told that it was a matter of economy, but that was nonsense because a Harley-Davidson with sidecar would consume more gas than a typical scout car in the same period of time. Anyway, I grew to hate the damned things and could hardly wait till I would be done with them.

My reprieve was slow coming, and I spent all of the winter and part of the spring riding the monsters and performing the duties typically assigned to cadets: looking after school crossings, doing house checks for people away on vacation, and being a general dogsbody for the rest of the division. It was for the most part very boring, and I found myself inventing ways to amuse myself.

During our training, we had learned how to cause the sidecar wheel to lift off the ground and remain suspended in the air. I became very proficient at this trick and was obsessed with seeing how long I could go before I was compelled to let it drop back down onto to the pavement. Sometimes I would travel in this manner for very long periods of time, often madly careening through complete subdivisions with my scarf flying behind me my and sidecar suspended at a forty-five-degree angle, its wheel spinning in the breeze.

I can't imagine what people in the area thought was going on, I guess I didn't care.

One day as I was doing one of my routine house checks, I noticed some footprints in the fresh snow leading to the rear of one of the fancy homes on the Bridle Path. I followed them till they ended in a packed-down area opposite an open basement window.

I was just about to go forward to have a look in when a pillowcase came flying out of the opening. As it landed on the ground, several pieces of silverware spilled out into the snow. A second full pillowcase followed, and then the arms and upper torso of a very large man began to emerge.

He was still struggling to drag himself through the small opening when I moved over and positioned myself directly in front of and above him.

He saw my boots and then slowly looked up at me. "Shit," he said with a defeated look on his face.

I thought I better restrain him before he got up, so I knelt on his back while he obligingly surrendered his wrists.

They were so thick I had trouble getting my cuffs on them, and when I grabbed his arms to help him to his feet, my hands were having trouble spanning his biceps.

I pushed him in front of me till we got to my motorcycle and had him kneel down facing away from me while I called for a scout car to come and get him.

I tried several times to reach the dispatcher, but the radio had decided, as it frequently did in those days, not to work.

There were no telephones readily available, so I decided to break the rules and take him to the station in my sidecar.

It wasn't easy cramming his bulk into that tiny capsule, but for some reason he remained cooperative and I got him in and secure. He rode quietly on the way to the lockup, with his head held down in shame and turned away from me.

I needed the help of two other officers to pry him out of the sidecar and get him into the interrogation room and into the hands of an investigating detective. I was going to leave and have my lunch, but the detective said he wanted me to stay while he talked to the prisoner.

It was really hot and stuffy in the little room, so I decided to make myself more comfortable. The prisoner, for the first time really looking at me, watched, astonished, as I peeled layer after layer of heavy clothing off, eventually revealing my true size and stature.

He just sat shaking his head for a while, and then turned to the detective and said, "I can't believe I let that scrawny little prick bring me in here."

4: Meeting Maloney

Policemen have several different uniforms. In my day, we had one for each season of the year. On any given day every cop in the city had to be dressed in the same outfit, and when there's a change in the weather it's his responsibility to find out what the dress of the day is and show up for work properly attired.

The officers in charge, many of whom were ex-military types, were real sticklers on this rule. It wasn't uncommon for guys who showed up with the wrong uniform, to be sent home and docked a day's pay.

I knew all this and that's why I was so nervous when I arrived at my first posting after Police College. The thing is, the weather had changed, and we all were supposed to be wearing winter pea jackets, but I hadn't been issued with one. I hoped that the sergeant in charge would under-stand, but if he were anything like Sgt. Saul, my drill instructor at the col-lege, my career might be on hold before it even got started.

I didn't get a chance to talk to the sergeant before the detachment paraded for duty, so I found myself in the lineup, sticking out like a sore thumb in my summer uniform while everybody else was bundled up in heavy winter coats.

In an effort to be inconspicuous, I positioned myself at the end of the line of big cops. I hoped that I'd be able to discuss my situation discreetly with the sergeant when the inspection was over.

For a while, I wasn't drawing any undue attention, but then a door at the rear of the room burst open and a huge policeman made his way over to the lineup and stood right beside me. He was a mountain of a man, over six foot six, with broad shoulders, huge hands and arms that seemed ready to burst the sleeves of his coat. "I'm sorry to be late Sarge," he said in a thick Irish brogue.

I took half a step backwards hoping to hide myself in the big guy's shadow, but it was too late. The sergeant had spotted me.

He came over and stood in front me and at first he seemed to be about to say something to me, but then changed his mind and started to move away.

I was still breathing a sigh of relief when I felt a big hand on my shoulder and heard a voice bellow from somewhere up above me. It was my neighbour, and he was addressing the sergeant. "Excuse me, Sarge" he said, "I see that this little fella doesn't have a winter coat."

What a rat, I thought.

"Now I hate to see anybody go out in weather like this without a warm coat," the big guy continued. "I've got a spare one in me locker and the kid's welcome to it".

I tried to say, "Thanks, but that won't be necessary." but the sergeant, who seemed to be enjoying the situation, cut me short.

"That's very generous of you, Maloney," he said, and the two men exchanged knowing glances.

I tried to object while the big fellow went to his locker, but the sergeant raised a finger and hushed me.

Maloney arrived back with something large and blue draped over his arm. "Here, get into this, sonny." he said.

I tried to object again, but the look on the sergeant's face told me that my fate was sealed.

I looked like a small child trying on his father's coat: the sleeves hung down six inches beyond the ends of my hands and the neck and collar threatened to slip down over my shoulders. Everybody had a good laugh at my expense; I secretly vowed revenge.

After finding me a coat that actually fit, the sergeant sent me out to patrol on foot for the first half of my shift. I spent the four hours devising plans to get even with Maloney and hoping that I might encounter some criminal, preferably small, on whom I could take out

Patrick Maloney

some of the anger and embarrassment that I was feeling.

As it turned out my time on the beat that afternoon was uneventful.

I was hoping that the lunchroom would be empty when I came in to eat, but as I approached it I could hear the familiar sound of the dominoes swishing on the tabletops and the loud banter as the men played

Bump. The room sounded full, but one voice carried over all the others and it had a distinctively Irish flavor to it.

Okay, I'm not going to let him get to me, I thought, *I'll just go in there and mind my own business, eat my lunch and leave.*

I grabbed a seat at the far end of the table, away from the Bump players, and opened my old tin lunch box. I had just started to remove the waxed paper from one of the sandwiches that my first wife, Barb, had packed for me, when Maloney left the game and took a seat directly opposite to me.

I watched him inhale what was left of his lunch while I poured a cup of tea from my thermos and fiddled with my sandwiches; I had lost my appetite.

Maloney watched as I started to put the sandwich back into the lunch box. "Hoy! ain't you gonna eat dat?"

"Naw," I said. "I'm not hungry."

Then, hoping to ingratiate myself, I offered him the lunch that my wife had so lovingly prepared for my first day at work.

"Pass her over," he said, and then proceeded to wolf it down.

He wasn't long making his way through the first half of the sandwich; but as he bit into the second half and drew back something pulled out with the egg and mayonnaise.

It was a piece of paper.

He put the sandwich down, unfolded the paper, and wiped it off. I LOVE YOU, the note said.

"Jeezuz," said Maloney.

Of course, he wasn't hesitant in sharing the note with the other cops at the table, saying, "I tink da litter feller loiks me."

I just wanted lunch hour to be over so that I could get back out on the beat again, but before I could escape, the sergeant came over to me with the worst news possible.

"Maloney's partner has booked off sick and I want you to go out with him on the paddy wagon for the rest of the shift. "

At first I thought he was joking, but when Maloney came over and put his big arm around me and ushered me out the door, winking at the guys and saying, "Don't wait up for us, boys," I knew my hazing was not yet over.

When we got to the garage, I started to get into the passenger door of the wagon, but Maloney swung me around and said, "No, no you drive."

I tried to explain that I'd never driven a rig like that before, but he wouldn't listen and just kept pushing me towards the driver's door.

When I finally seated myself behind the wheel and had slid the seat as far forward as it would go, he started saying encouraging things to me like, "Can ya see over dat steering wheel, sonny?" and, "We'll get some blocks put on dose pedals for ya for da next trip."

Fortunately, I had not yet been issued a gun.

After we had toured around for a couple of hours, Maloney seemed to tire of all the teasing and tried having a normal conversation with me. When he asked me questions about myself, my answers were curt and guarded and I think he began to sense that for some reason I might be miffed with him.

He was silent for a while but then came out with what he thought was a brilliant idea. "Look, I knows I was a bit hard on you in front of the boys, but it was all in fun. So here's what we do. When we gets back to the station, I'll bug you some more, you act like you can't take it anymore and go for me and we'll tussle. We'll make it look real and I'll let you win; how's dat?"

"Oh, I don't know," I started to say, but he just punched me on the shoulder

"Good: dat's settled."

When we returned to the station, we had the first of what were to be-come regular mock wrestling matches that always ended in me getting the big ape into a submission hold and him begging for mercy. No one was fooled, of course, but it seemed to give Maloney no end of pleasure and, as for me, it was easier being part of a joke than it was being the brunt of one.

That didn't mean that he stopped having fun at my expense, but over time I began to get a clearer picture of the type of man he really was, and I took his jibes with grain of salt.

I sometimes I rode with him in the wagon, gathering drunks off the streets at closing time, and it wasn't unusual for him to deliver more of them to their doorsteps than he did to the drunk tank.

He was a great man in a scrap, because for the most part he didn't have to actually do anything; his size and obvious strength gave most troublemakers sober second thoughts. When it was required, I watched him lift large men, kicking and punching, off their feet and pitch them into the back of his wagon like they were so much cord wood; but I also saw him cradling a dead child in his arms at an accident scene, crying like she was his own. At heart, he was a big gentle man without a mean bone in his body.

We made quite a sight and turned more than a few heads when we walked the beat together, with the top of my hat travelling along at the same level as his shoulder flashes. Of course, it didn't help matters when he would stop and introduce me to store owners as his little friend, while patting my head.

I endured all the indignities in silence because I knew that when I was with him I could relax and not suffer the anxiety I experienced when I patrolled the same areas alone.

5: More Maloney baloney

You could join the force as a cadet at the age of eighteen, but as soon as you turned twenty-one you automatically became a full-fledged constable. By that time, you would, normally, have attended Police College and received the firearms training that would allow you to carry a service revolver.

As it happened, I was injured and in the hospital when it was time for me to take the training, so while I waited for the next class I was sent to one of toughest divisions in the city, unarmed and untrained. That's where I met Maloney. I sure appreciated having him around; he was a lot better weapon than my gun would have been.

Even though I didn't have a gun, I still had to comply with the uniform regulations and wear my full Sam Browne with holster and ammunition pouch. There was a problem with this arrangement, because when I sat down the empty holster would fold over and crack the leather. If I was one of the old hands this wouldn't have made much difference, but I was due to attend the next class at the college and that meant my kit would have to be in perfect condition. I remembered the trouble I got into with Sergeant Saul the drill instructor during cadet training and I didn't want a repeat performance.

I solved the problem of the folding holster by fashioning a supporting frame out of an old coat hanger. It was roughly the shape of the holster and fit neatly inside to hold its shape.

One day, when I was sitting in the guardroom with Maloney, me touching up my leather, I pulled the wire frame out and he said, "What's with the sling shot?"

I hadn't thought of it before, but it did look just like a little slingshot.

"Gimme dat," he said and whipped it out of my hand. He pulled open a desk drawer, found some rubber bands and strung them across the frame. "There ya go," he said. "Now you're armed."

One thing led to another, and soon we were taking turns firing tiny bits of folded paper at the framed photograph of Commissioner Bick that hung on the wall of the lunchroom.

As time went on, whenever things got boring in the station, the big Irishman would insist that I haul out my slingshot so we could have another go at the Commissioner. Because of his frequent requests I got in the habit of keeping a good supply of paper wads in my ammunition pouch.

Maloney and I were out on patrol in a scout car on the late shift when the radio lit up with a call reporting an armed robbery. As the dispatcher described the person responsible, we realized that we were already looking at a man who fit the description perfectly. We had noticed him jogging along the sidewalk beside us and now, as we sped up to get a better look, he took off in full flight.

Maloney was at the wheel and I was riding shotgun, inappropriate somehow since I didn't have one. We overtook the bandit easily, but he suddenly dodged into a narrow alley where the car couldn't follow.

Maloney hit the brakes and shouted for me to chase the man on foot while he drove around the block to try to cut him off. I was out of the car like a shot and as I started up the alley I heard Maloney shouting, "Wait, I forgot you don't have—"

It was too late I had the scent and there was no stopping me. I lost sight of the man momentarily as he turned into a large service lane, but as I rounded the corner I could see that the distance was closing and that it wouldn't be long before I caught up with him.

When I was almost up to him he swung to his right into another alley. Just then my boot hit something and I tripped and stumbled forward.

When I regained my balance and turned the corner I could see that we were in a short, dead-end alley blocked at the far end by a twelve-foot-high chain link fence.

My man had climbed almost to the top and his feet were just out of reach when I arrived at the bottom of the fence and made a mad grab for them. My boots weren't made for climbing and he was about to get away, so I went to plan B.

"Stop or I'll blow your bloody brains out," I growled in my best 'Dirty Harry' voice.

Wow! It worked, and from the way he smelt when he let go and dropped in front of me, I had literally scared the shit out of him.

"Keep your hands on the fence and spread em," I said, and then started to search him.

The scout cars headlights illuminated us both as Maloney swung into the lane behind me.

When I heard the big guy open his door and start puffing his way towards us I leaned forward and hissed into the bad guy's ear, "Turn around slowly and don't try anything. I've got you covered."

When Maloney got to me I was standing with my fully loaded sling-shot pointed at the bad guy.

"Jeezuz!" said Maloney.

"Jeezuz!" said the bad guy.

6: Small fry

Being one of the smallest guys on the job, I was like a magnet for every thug who wanted to have a go at assaulting a policeman. In the past I had always adhered to the policy that "It's a poor set of feet the lets your nose get in trouble", but I couldn't run away anymore. I relied heavily on my gift of the gab, but when that failed I would have to mix it up as best I could. These encounters left me stiff and bruised and cost the city a lot of money replacing torn uniforms.

Whenever Maloney arrived to find me struggling away with some big guy, he would give me a wink and then fire my assailant into the back of the wagon, saying, "Why don't you pick on somebody your own size?'

I was alone late one night, walking the beat on King St. in the heart of the city; it was a drizzly fall night and I had stopped in the shelter of a doorway to update my memo book. It was well past bar closing time and the city was shutting down.

An empty streetcar pulled up and opened its doors at a stop directly in front of me. I stepped forward and exchanged a few words with a tired-looking conductor who was heading to the barn at the end his shift, then backed into the doorway to finish my writing.

I stayed put a while longer; trying to shake off the sleepiness that was taking hold of me, then decided to move on. As I stepped out of the door-way and looked to my right I noticed a strange form in the distance mov-ing toward me. I moved back into the doorway and removed my hat so I could peer around and get a better look.

At first it appeared to be a large man some distance away, but when I looked more closely I realized that it was a very small man more close at hand. In fact he was a dwarf, and as I watched him tack his way up the sidewalk, I realized that he was a very drunk.

I reclaimed my spot in the shadowy doorway and waited for him to pass, but instead of moving on by, he stopped directly in front of me and started digging in his pockets for streetcar tokens. He was very unsteady on his feet and only managed to stay upright by wrapping his stubby arms around a convenient lamppost.

I was just about to go and help him when another streetcar pulled up and the doors whooshed open.

The little fellow left the security of his post, staggered to the trolley and tried to climb aboard. The step up to the car was about waist high on him and he made several abortive attempts to mount them; the last time taking a run at them and landing on his back.

I rushed over to him, helped him into a sitting position and asked him if he was hurt. He just giggled and mumbled something incomprehensible; it was obvious that he was feeling no pain.

When I asked the conductor if he would help me get him aboard, he made it perfectly clear to me that he was not going to be responsible for looking after the little guy. I told him that if he didn't I would have to call for the wagon, but he didn't seem to care. Actually, I knew it might not be that serious because Maloney was driving that night.

After picking the man up and dusting him off I carried him into my doorway and propped him against the wall. Then walked the short distance to the call box and requested some transportation.

I knew the wagon was close by so I went back and hustled my prisoner over to the curb so that we would be easy to spot. That's when inspiration struck!

When Maloney arrived I was standing, all puffed up and proud, with my nightstick in one hand and my prisoner handcuffed to my opposite wrist.

Maloney stuck his head out of the wagon window and said, "I think you better throw that one back."

7: Ladies of the night

In 1964 the Police Department decided to make a special effort to reduce the number of women employed in 'the world's oldest profession'. It may have become a priority because the frat houses at the University of Toronto were starting to use the services of these shady ladies quite frequently, often including them as part of their initiations and hazings. Many of the civic fathers had their sons attending the university and were anxious to see that the reputations of their privileged offspring remained unsullied.

The Morality Squad selected several new recruits, fresh out of Police College, to assist them in their quest to rid the city of these wicked women, and I was among the chosen few. They wanted us to pose as university students and participate in a scheme that today would be considered entrapment; but back then 'all was fair in illicit love and war/'

Our job was to head down into the tenderloin districts of the city and wait until we were solicited by one of the hookers. The job didn't end there. We were issued with marked money and instructed to go with the woman in question to her room. When she had disrobed to the extent that there could be no mistaking her purpose and had accepted the marked money. we were instructed to whip out our badges and arrest them.

At first the women were pretty easy to trick. Although we didn't have the academic qualifications, with our Ivy League togs and haircuts we could pass well enough as students. There were no entrance exams.

Several of my young classmates who were assigned the same duties had, at the outset, been very apprehensive about how the prostitutes would react when they found out that they had been duped. At a general meeting before we started the operation they expressed the concern that they would be unarmed and that some of these girls were pretty tough.

I, however, was not worried and, before I realized what I was doing, blurted out that, in my opinion, the women would simply surrender gracefully and accept the situation as just another part of the job.

The room fell silent for what seemed a long time and I was getting some strange looks, especially from the Morality Squad detectives. I knew they wanted me to explain how it was that I knew so much about prostitutes, but they let it slide and continued with the briefing. The American military's rule of 'Don't ask and don't tell' is not a new concept.

The fact was that I did know a lot about prostitutes. Now, don't get me wrong. It's just that you can't have lived on Pembroke Street in downtown Toronto in the 1950s and passed the Spot One Grill on Dundas Street every morning on the way to school and not have learned a great deal about these ladies of the night.

Now, as I sat with the rest of the cops planning our assault on the bawdy business, it occurred to me that the girls in the business must be hurting already. It was the era of free love, and who could compete with that?

But duty is duty, so I played the game and did what I was told.

It was a short assignment. After a couple of arrests, the girls all knew me and I had to be replaced.

I was right about their attitude. They couldn't have cared less: the arrest and the fine were just the cost of doing business. Both the girls whom I temporarily removed from the streets found the situation hilariously funny and we had a good laugh together before I took them in. Of course, they felt compelled to embarrass me in front of the Desk Sergeant by offering me a freebie but that, for want of a less explicit phrase, was just a little tit for tat.

Actually, they bore me no grudge and later, when I was patrolling the streets in uniform and they were back in business, they would often greet me like an old friend.

8: The nicest little whorehouse on Pembroke Street

Kids will be kids, no matter where they live or who their parents are. When I was a ten-year-old boy living in the slums of Toronto, some of my best friends came from families whose occupations were not always on the right side of the law. But in our little world that didn't seem to matter.

Of my three closest friends there was Marvin, whose father was a receiver of stolen goods and kept a still in his basement; Nick, whose father was a bootlegger with mafia connections; and, last but not least, there was Terry, whose mother owned a special kind of rooming house across the road from where I lived.

As kids growing up in a notorious area on the verges of Cabbage Town, we saw a lot but at our age understood very little. Terry and I, like the other kids in the neighbourhood, spent a lot of time participating in all the normal local after-school pursuits like snaring pigeons in Allan Gardens or dragging big magnets up and down the back lanes to see what rusty treasures we could snag.

As kids will, we had sleepovers. Terry spent nights at my house, but I liked it best when we stayed at his place. It was more fun.

His house was a real hive of activity. He had several aunts who lived in the rooms upstairs and there were all kinds of interesting men coming to visit them. It was as if there were a party going on all the time and, best of all, his aunts were always subsidizing our banana splits at the Chinese restaurant on the corner if we promised to stay there for an hour or so.

After Terry, Nick, and I joined the Boy Scouts, we got into the habit of going to Terry's house after our Wednesday-night meetings to have some hot chocolate and finish off the evening with a game of Monopoly. We always played at a table located in a kitchen at the rear of the house.

It must have been disconcerting for the visiting men to see us huddled around the table in our green shirts and blue shorts, with our Stetsons tilted back on our heads. They would come strutting down the stairs from the second floor with cocky, satisfied looks on their faces, but when they spied our little Scout troop, they'd quickly hustle off looking confused and guilty.

Terry's aunts sure had a lot of friends coming and going and, strangely, many of them were Chinese. I felt that that was a little unusual, but I had become accustomed to seeing unusual things around Terry's house.

One day when I was about to start up the stairs to the second-floor bathroom, I was confronted by a legless man swinging down the stairs towards me, using his arms to propel himself in a sort of hopping motion. I say 'legless', but actually his body seemed to end at the base of his rib cage, and the way he moved put me in mind of some sort of giant insect.

I returned to the kitchen and told Terry about what I had seen, but he just shrugged and explained that the man's name was John and that whenever the circus was in town he came and visited his aunts. Then Terry pulled a fistful of free carnival tickets out of his pocket and waved them in my face saying, "Look what he gave me."

Terry and I and two younger boys who also lived in the house took the streetcar to the Canadian National Exhibition the following day and had a great time on the midway. We ended our day touring the freak show, spending most of our time in front of Kandar The Human Torso, with whom we exchanged knowing winks.

There was always something exciting happening at Terry's house. One evening the three of us were sitting quietly in the kitchen after our Scout meeting when we heard a loud bang and a crash as the front door caved in. Then a man came running down from the second floor, taking the stairs two at a time. He was given chase by several uniformed policemen who were pouring through the gap where the front door had been. They all made their way down the hall past where we were sitting ... first the man from upstairs and then the cops in hot pursuit.

The fugitive brushed past us and made it out the back door, then leapt over the porch rail and ran through the back yard. We leaned over the table to protect the game board as the policemen, looking like a version of the Keystone Cops, elbowed their way into the room, crowded through the back door, then bunched up on the narrow porch. Two of the officers drew their guns and fired several warning shots, then the whole group clambered down the back stairs and continued the chase.

Nick and I got up from our chairs and watched the group disappear in the distance, but Terry remained at the table calm and unimpressed. I think he used the opportunity to move his marker to a better location on the game board.

In truth, it wasn't always fun and games around the place. One day as we sat on the front porch, we saw a cop chasing a man down the sidewalk on the opposite side of the street. The policeman was losing ground, so he stopped and threw his nightstick at the guy who was getting away.

He missed, but a garbage man who was perched leveling trash on the top of a dump truck parked by the curb. leveling trash, saw what was going on and decided to intervene. As the man passed him he swung his heavy shovel down and struck the fleeing man on the head, stopping him literally dead in his tracks.

We watched as the policeman and the truck driver leaned over the motionless man while a puddle of blood gradually formed around his head. Shortly a little Italian lady from a nearby house came over, shoved them aside, then made a little tent with a newspaper and placed it over the man's his lifeless face.

The saddest thing that ever occurred at the house, and the main reason I stopped spending time there, occurred during the summer of 1955. Terry and the other kids at the house had been away for about two weeks when one afternoon he showed up at my place with tears in his eyes, telling me that David, an eight-year-old son of one of his aunts, had drowned while swimming.

They had been vacationing at Wasaga Beach, where his mother kept a summer cottage. Terry often invited me to join them there, but I never did. My parents, who were working very hard and were often away, had no idea what was going on at Terry's house and I didn't want to press my luck. They might have wanted to meet his mum before allowing me to travel that far away with them.

When I heard about what happened to poor little David, I was glad I hadn't been there to witness it. I attended the funeral for a short time, but after seeing the little fellow dressed in a tux lying in a small coffin, looking more like a puppet than a person, I couldn't take it.

I can still see Terry's aunts, dressed in unaccustomed black, clustered around the tiny coffin, weeping. I didn't know what to say or how to act, so I just walked away, vowing never to attend another funeral and, with a couple of exceptions, I never have.

I didn't blame anybody at the house for the boy's death. The kids there were watched over more closely than I was. Terry's mother and aunts, when not engaged in their nocturnal pursuits, were normal, caring people, but somehow I couldn't face being in the house anymore.

Shortly after the boy's death we moved from the neighbourhood. As I grew older I, of course, realized what had been going on in Terry's house...you can't have lived on Pembroke St. and not have known. During the late 1950s, that area was the epicentre of Toronto's flesh trade, surpassing even the infamous Jarvis St.

Terry's mothers place was not the only residence on our block that sported a red light in the window, but I can testify from personal experience that it was the nicest little whorehouse on the street.

The corner of Pembroke and Dundas

9: Prisoner sandwiches

They're just fried egg sandwiches: buttered white bread, egg hard over, the yolk broken and lots of salt and pepper—simple fare but much appreciated in my house. I first encountered this delicacy over fifty years ago when I was working as a police cadet, serving at 57 Division in downtown Toronto.

That location had the distinction of being the city's sole repository for female felons. The building had the standard floor plan for lockups of the period: a large, dank, high-ceilinged, gymnasium-like area with a sizable central portion encased in bars, surrounded by small individual cells. At all the other stations in the city the bigger area was referred to as the bull pen...the insensitive old regulars at our station called it the cow pen or, when there was a particularly large consignment of younger hookers, the heifer pen.

When I first arrived at the division and heard these references, I felt that those who were serving there were being unnecessarily vulgar, since they were dealing with the weaker sex. I wasn't long learning that working with male prisoners was a walk in the park compared to looking after their female counterparts. Never then and never since have I encountered a baser, more debauched, more violent segment of society, particularly those women destined for the 'drunk tank'.

I got my first clue of what was in store for me while parading for duty on my first evening shift. There was a long, narrow room adjacent to the garage where all of us, constables and cadets alike, were lined up for inspection before hitting the streets.

The regulations required that we all stand at attention in a long row, forearms raised with gun in one hand and memo book in the other. We had to hold that stance until the attending sergeant finished his inspection and dismissed us.

It was while we were suspended in this position that a paddy wagon backed into the garage and offloaded a cargo of some mature ladies of the night. The sergeant, distracted, failed to say, "As you were," so we were left hanging, no pun intended, as the women filed in.

Encouraged by a boisterous, grey-haired, veteran floozy, each woman, in turn, groped our crotches and offered disparaging criticisms as they passed by.

While I was being subjected to this indignity, I turned my attention to a large, framed print hanging on the wall we smirking cops were facing. It was a colourful cartoon print entitled the "Ascent of Venus." It depicted several Keystone type cops carrying an stereotypical aging old-time prostitute up jailhouse stairs. It set the tone of the place.

Apparently, to survive and maintain my sanity in this environment, I was going to have to develop a perverse sense of humour.

That initiation was a harbinger of things to come. The first time I was detailed to remain inside and monitor the cells I entered the area hoping to initiate a firm, but fair and friendly, rapport. This approach was short-lived.

As I got to the first individual cell and looked in, a woman who had been lying on the hard metal shelf that served as a bed threw the army blanket that had been covering her off, revealing that she was totally naked. She then rushed towards the bars that separated us, grabbed hold of them and proceeded to perform a lewd dance.

Astonished and embarrassed, I beat a retreat and, red-faced, went to the desk sergeant to report the incident.

"Sergeant, there's a naked lady in there," I stammered.

Peering over his glasses with feigned concern on his face he replied, "You don't say. Well, we can't have any behaviour of that sort in an establishment like this. You better take me in there at once."

I escorted him in.

After staring at the woman for some time he simply said, "Yup, she's naked, all right, and she also seems to be double jointed."

Then he went away.

Several more constables ventured in to watch her perform and establish the fact that she was indeed naked. Then one of them took me aside and whispered in my ear, "Grow up, sonny!"

I guess, after a time, I did. I got used to the dishevelled, bruised bodies lying sprawled on the floor of the drunk tank. I became adept at ducking the spit and sometimes feces that were flung at me through the bars. I listened to what seemed like a whole new vocabulary of profanity, familiar words that somehow seemed different and dirtier when hurled from a woman's mouth.

Mercifully, female minors were not exposed to that environment. There were facilities for juveniles across town, and a room upstairs in the station for the more sensitive customers.

One of my jobs was to maintain a constant flow of the thick, bitter-tasting coffee that was offered to the prisoners in the hopes that they would be sober enough to face the magistrate the following day.

Since it was a bed and breakfast of sorts, we also offered a limited menu to see them on their way to court in the morning. One fried egg sandwich and nothing else.

There was a Greek restaurant across the road from the station that catered the daily event. In truth, the cuisine at the establishment was not totally unpalatable. When the orders were placed in the morning, some-times the number of sandwiches accidentally exceeded the number of prisoners present and the cops would have to take up the slack.

And that was where I acquired a fondness for Prisoner Sandwiches, as they were called, particularly if I could select ones that were not liberally sprinkled with ash from the cigarette that was ever-present, hanging from the old chef's mouth.

My wife, Andrea, was an early convert to this comfort food, and one by one my kids have followed suit. You can't order prisoner sandwiches by name at any restaurant, and if you could explain and get a specially-pre-pared substitute, it wouldn't taste quite like the ones I make at home. The watery, pale-yoked commercial eggs of those establishments don't hold a candle to the ones produced by our free- range chickens; and to be fully appreciated, the sandwiches need to be consumed in a kitchen warmed by a cook stove with just a hint of wood smoke wafting around, and the air buzzing with family chatter.

10: Sleeping with the Beatles

Somehow I survived my unarmed sojourn at 52 Division and made it to the Academy for my formal training. Things went quite smoothly during the weeks I spent there; and all my apprehensions about meeting the notorious Sergeant Saul again were unfounded. He was still the gruff old curmudgeon I remembered, but as he had a go at me and the other guys in the class I was sure he had his tongue in his cheek.

When he paraded us for duty on the second-to-last day of the course, he had some surprise information for us. "I've got some good news and some bad news for you," he said. "The good news is that you guys are getting out of here a day early. The bad news is that you are all going downtown to guard a bunch of rock and roll fairies with hair down to their arses. They're called the Bugs or something."

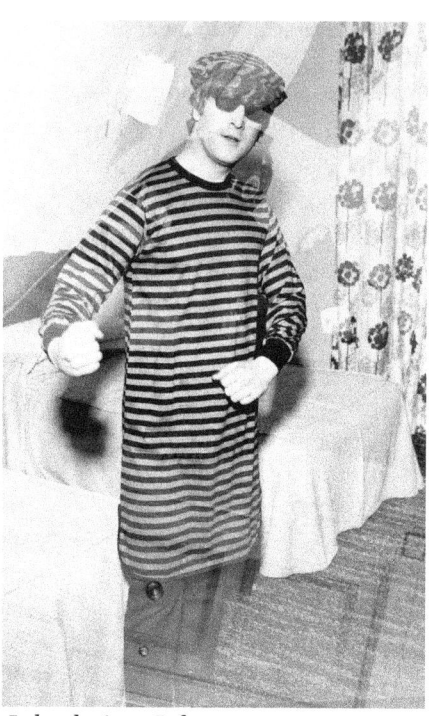

John being John

Although we were all young men and women, only a few of us had heard of the Beatles, and those who claimed to know their music were immediately suspect. We were ordered to show up early the following morning and be prepared for an extra-long shift.

It didn't seem like a good way to begin a police career. I didn't want to be a bodyguard; I wanted to be on the street catching criminals and suppressing crime.

Then things got worse. When the duties were handed out I learned that I wasn't even going to be on the street with the rest of my classmates. I had drawn the short straw and was doomed to spend two days and nights in the Empire Suite of the King Edward Hotel, looking after some weirdo guys from Britain. I had no idea what they looked or sounded like, and I didn't care.

I was at the hotel early that day, patrolling the halls and keeping everybody off the private floor designated for the band's use.

In the early afternoon something very strange happened. I was still inside, and I felt something change before I actually saw or heard anything; the atmosphere suddenly became charged with excitement.

When I went to a window to see what was going on I couldn't believe my eyes. The streets were plugged with people for as far as the eye could see; all traffic had come to a standstill and the pressure of the bulging crowd threatened to push the store windows in. I could see my classmates laughing and joking with the kids in the crowd; everybody was excited and happy, not at all like the situations described in our training. They were all having fun and I was stuck in the stuffy old hotel.

Sergeant Crawford, the officer in charge of the detail inside the hotel, slapped me on the back and shook me out of my reverie. "Get down to the front door and help get those buggers inside!"

By the time I got to the doors and made my way out to join the dozen or so huge cops waiting outside, things had reached fever pitch. The patrol sergeant shouted over the noise of the crowd, "Form a semicircle in front of the doors and lock your arms."

Members of the Mounted unit, on excited prancing horses, parted the crowd for a long procession of police vehicles, followed by a paddy wagon. The big beige van backed into the secure area we had held in front of the hotel and its back door flew open.

I only got a quick look at the Beatles as they leapt from the wagon and dashed for the hotel lobby, because a surge of crowd pressure hit our protective circle and I snapped up into the air, suspended between the big guys on either side of me.

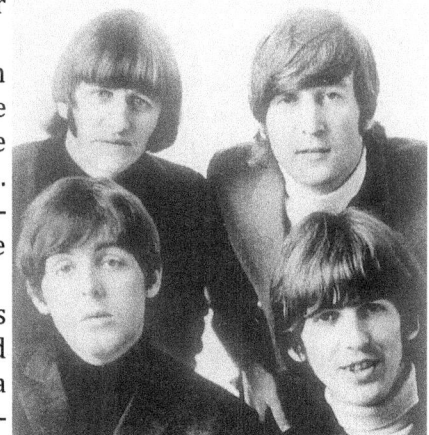

The Fab Four

An enterprising young girl in a white angora sweater attempted to crawl under my dangling legs to get at the band, but I locked them around her and held in a scissor hold till the boys were safely inside.

45

It took quite a bit of brushing to get the white hairs off the ass of my pants when things settled down.

I broke ranks with the group of huge cops outside and followed a separate bunch as they escorted the band members through the crowded lobby and over to a bank of elevators. It was pandemonium; the doors to the lifts hadn't opened as planned and women were pushing by me and flinging themselves kamikaze-like up and over the wall of policemen.

I spotted Sergeant Crawford in front of an elevator away from the main bank; he was holding the door open and waving me over to him.

I got there as quickly as I could, and when we pushed the up button and the doors started to close I could see that the battle in front of the other elevators was still going on.

We arrived at the private floor, had a quick look around, then stood by and waited for the other elevators to arrive.

Eventually the doors opened, and a screen of policemen parted to reveal four bony young men with long hair and tight pants. They looked like they were having a terrific time as they emerged, breathless, laughing, fiddling with their hair and straightening their clothes.

The whole group brushed passed me and hurried down the hall to their suite, and as the door closed I said to myself, My work here is finished.

It was the end of my shift, so I took advantage of the lull to make up my memo book while I waited for my relief to arrive.

That's when things went from bad to worse.

Sergeant Crawford came back down the hall with his band of big cops in tow, and I watched as he directed them over to the stair well and sent them on their way. I knew I was in for it when he came over to me and put his arm around my shoulder and started to speak in a low voice.

"Listen, son, the band manager complained about all the big guys guarding the boys. He says that they were feeling intimidated and starting to refer to, them as the goon squad. I'm putting them down in the lobby and you, my little friend, are going to spend the night with the band."

There was nothing I could do about, it so I found a phone and tried to explain that I couldn't come home because I had to spend the night in the Empire Suite with a rock and roll band.

So, there it was, just me, Sergeant. Crawford and the Beatles. At least, that's the way it was supposed to be.

The Beatles, a name I was now able to remember, were by this time settled in and running in and out of their rooms in their underwear, with drinks in their hands. I took up a position in an easy chair in a corner of the living room while Sergeant Crawford acted as bartender. I was frequently on my feet, answering the door and admitting throngs of strange people: show biz types, reporters, hookers, and more.

In addition to these invited guests, we had visits from all kinds of kids who made incredibly creative attempts to get close to these guys who seemed to be their idols.

One of the better attempts was made by a young man who had looted the laundry chute for a bus boy uniform and picked up a discarded coffee pot and tray from outside of one of the rooms. He was brazenly making his way into the suite as if on room service when I unintentionally touched the coffee pot. it was ice cold, and when I took a closer look at him I could see his jeans and sandals underneath the white hotel uniform.

I let him have a good look at the guys and then escorted him out of the room.

There were many similar incidents and the people whom I turned away, many of whom were staying at the hotel, spread the word that I was staying in the Beatles' suite. Whenever I went down to the lobby or the restaurant I was mobbed by kids, mostly girls, who would heap me with gifts that they had made for the various members of the band.

Streets were jammed with fans

I took the presents to the suite and added them to the growing heap of unopened offerings already there. When I went back down to the lobby I made up stories about how well they were received.

At one point I felt particularly imposed upon when the band's manager recruited me to participate in a little production line he was setting up. He had the boys sitting side by side on a sofa and they were adding their signatures to small squares of paper and passing them one to the other until they reached me. I was seated next to a guy who said his name was Ringo Starr, I thought he was putting me on, but that was the way he signed the paper.

It was my job to gather up the autographs and arrange them in piles of ten and put an elastic band around each bundle. This process went on for quite a while and when I became bored and started adding my signature to the last few papers to reach me.

We all had a laugh and the manager tossed me a large pile for myself. I gave most of them away to the fans in the lobby and the remainder, later on, to friends and relatives who seemed interested. I kept one or two for myself but have long since lost track of them.

One of the Beatles told the sergeant that he had relatives in the city and that he would like to visit them. We devised a plan that got him out of the hotel and back again safely. I think it was George Harrison, but at the time I wasn't sufficiently impressed with them to remember who was who.

After twenty-four hours of nonstop excitement—I don't know when anyone slept—I have to admit that I was starting to enjoy myself and I kind of missed the boys when they went off to perform at Maple Leaf Gardens.

After all that time I was in sore need of a shave and a change of clothes. I didn't think that any of their gear would fit me, but I did accept a disposable razor and some tooth paste from John Lennon.

By the time the Beatles were scheduled to leave the city, the crowd of admirers had grown to such huge proportions that the Chief of Police, James Mackey, decided to take personal charge of the special operation to remove them from the hotel. Since Sergeant Crawford and I were most familiar with the boys, we were included as integral parts of the plan.

When the time for the band's departure arrived, the chief called eight of the biggest men on the force into a huddle beside the elevators in the hall of the private floor.

"Here's how it's going to work," he said. "The wagon is standing by outside the front doors and I've got enough men on foot and on horses to keep the crowd back while we load these buggers. Our job is to get them through the lobby and over to the doors.

"The trouble is," he continued, "I just came up from there and the place is crammed with crazy teenagers. So, here's what we're going to do.

You eight men will take the elevator on the left down to the lobby. I'll wait with the band, Sergeant Crawford and little guy for precisely two minutes, and then we will take the next elevator down to join you. In the meantime, I want you boys to move over and form a V in front of our elevator so that when we get down there, we can get in behind while you push your way to the doors. Has everybody got that? Good. Synchronize your watches."

By the time he had finished his instructions the boys in the band had joined us and he set the plan in motion.

Down went the goon squad in elevator number one, then we entered elevator number two and I held the doors from closing while watching my watch. When exactly two minutes had passed the chief gave me the nod, I released the doors, and we were off.

In a matter of seconds, we reached the lobby and the doors opened. Instead of the protective wall of blue backs we expected we found ourselves all alone facing an enormous crowd of fans. The big cops had been delayed somehow.

We couldn't turn back now. At first I thought we would be mobbed, but for some reason nobody was reacting to our presence. I think they may have been confused because of all the Beatles imitators who had been hanging around the hotel, or maybe they simply couldn't believe their eyes.

It looked like we might get away without too much fuss and the chief said, "Let's ease our way over to the door."

Everything was going smoothly, too smoothly!

Ringo heading for the paddy wagon

I noticed an older woman half-way across the lobby staring wide eyed, with her mouth open. She was looking directly at Ringo Starr and I don't think at that point that she was sure that it was really him.

If he had left well enough alone we might have made it to the door un-scathed. Instead, the little bugger started shaking his tie at her and making lewd gestures.

That was it. She responded by launching herself across the lobby, leaping on his back, wrapping her legs around his waist and holding his tie like a set of reins.

I tried, but I couldn't dislodge her, so I pushed them both towards the door.

The chief had already ushered the rest of the group to the safety of a space between the ho-tel's double doors, where more policemen waited.

The cops on the other side of the door grabbed Ringo and dragged him through while I put a half nelson on the excited lady and gradually got her to dismount.

She was down but she wasn't out because, even though the door had closed between them, she still held Ringo's tie in a death grip. It was stuck between the doors and Ringo's face was flattened against the glass and turning colour.

Before I could react, a quick-thinking policeman on the other side of the glass produced a jackknife and cut the tie off. The lady fell backwards into the crowd with her memento, and I never saw her again.

The padd wagon departed by the crowd stayed on. Something very special and exciting had been happening and they didn't want it to end.

I felt the same way. On the way home I stopped and bought a Beatles album. I;ve been a fan ever since.

11: The Night Shift

As I was going up the stair
I met a man who wasn't there
He wasn't there again today
I wish, I wish he'd stay away
—Hughes Mearns

There's something terribly unnatural about being awake all night. Man is not a nocturnal animal.

All this nonsense of night shifts only started because of the arrival of the industrial age and its demands for more and more production time. Greedy mill owners forcing an unwilling third of their work force to adapt their normal body rhythms so they could function during those ungodly hours. Since the invention of artificial light, a race of pasty-faced mortals has evolved who willingly function and sometimes thrive during these dark hours.

I am not one of these people. My ancestors were people of the land, as my Dad used to say. They worked from "can't see to can't see". Surely those are sufficient hours spent awake and busy.

As strongly as I was opposed to working the night shift I knew that if I chose to continue pretending to be a policeman I would eventually be asked to drag my old metal lunch box into the station around midnight and stagger around the darkened city streets till eight the following morning.

When I first signed on as a cadet and was working at a station in the suburbs, I only worked during the day, but that coddling ceased after I received some formal training at the Police College and was assigned to 52 Division in the heart of the city.

I wasn't thrust immediately out of the sunlight and into the depths of darkness; the change was gradual. First they assigned me work during the afternoon, hoping I would be tricked into looking forward to the graveyard shift. They knew the most interesting and exciting times for a city policeman are the couple of hours immediately before and after midnight, and that I would be finishing my evenings on a high and looking for more action.

For some reason the population has reserved this pocket of time to concentrate their bad behaviour. The bars are closing, and the drunks are hitting the streets, couples have finally had enough of casual bickering and settled into some real knock- down, drag out domestic violence, robbers, muggers, break and enter men, and sexual offenders have slithered out of their daytime hideouts and the whole city is abuzz and frantic.

The Department's plan worked. All that excitement seduced me into thinking that I might actually enjoy the night shift. What I didn't realize was that as quickly as the city ramps up its midnight fervour, it also winds it down and, with the exception of a few tense moments just after that witching hour, most nights are spent in interminable groggy boredom.

For me, the worst hours were from about five o'clock in the morning until eight. I fought sleep all night but, even with the gallons of free coffee I consumed at the all-night restaurants, during those final hours my body was ready to give up the fight.

Near the end of my first midnight shift I was standing in front of a store on Young Street, watching the city come to life. It was about seven in the morning and the streetcars and buses were spewing out hordes of fresh-faced people heading for their sensible day jobs. I stood semi-comatose, propped up against a plate glass window, and not even the sight of the mini skirted secretaries descending from the trolley stairs was sufficient to arouse me from my stupor.

Suddenly all resistance failed me, and I actually fell dead asleep on my feet. Eyes closed, chin resting my chest, I fell back and slid slowly down the store window until my ass struck the cement sill and I was immediately jolted to full consciousness.

My collapse had not gone unnoticed. As I struggled back to my feet and dusted myself off, I was confronted by several concerned-looking citizens clustered around me. One older man in a neat business suit asked if I was all right, then leaned in close to my face while I replied. I think he thought he would smell booze on my breath, but when he didn't, he just walked away shaking his head.

I didn't know what to say to the rest of the people, so I just smiled- straightened my hat and wandered away chanting *fuck, fuck, fuck, fuck,*

fuck to myself.

I know it's telling tales out of school, but I feel compelled to confess that, shortly after that incident, I was taken aside by a couple of older officers, who shall remain anonymous, and given some essential tips on how to survive the rigours of the night and emerge semi well-rested.

If you were paired up in a scout car, you and your partner could take turns napping. If you were alone in a car, there were several locations in the division that the Patrol Sergeants were unaware of, where you could snooze with impunity. This meant that you must still be aware of and responsive to the police radio while you slept, but after a while this became second nature.

There were washrooms in certain office buildings that were open all night, where a beat cop could catch a couple of winks if he was careful. The trick was to nap sitting with your back propped up against the inside of the entrance door, so anybody trying to enter would bump you awake, and you could leap to your feet and greet him as if nothing had happened.

There were also certain residences in the area where understanding young ladies would stand guard while a hard-working officer had a well-deserved rest. This option, however, was reserved for a privileged few and the demands made in return for the hospitality given often left the recipient more tired when he left than when he arrived.

Sometimes we were paired up with other cops when we patrolled in scout cars, but when we walked the beat we were almost always alone. For some reason I wasn't afraid of the real dangers that I encountered in those dark city streets. Maybe it was because I had grown up in the midst of the danger and turmoil of the inner city and, for the most part, knew how to deal with it.

There was also the effect the police uniform had on me; it was in a sense my magic cloak and when I had it on I felt taller and stronger. I had my tense moments and on several occasions drew my gun in anger, but for the most part I was relaxed and confident when doing my job.

No, it wasn't the real tangible dangers that made me uneasy during those long lonely nights. It was an embarrassing fear of a phantom who had been stalking me since I was a kid, back in Saskatchewan. He only appeared when I was asleep or on the edge of sleep, but during the midnight shift he had ample opportunity to plague me. My sister Janis had scared the hell out of me with tales of the Bogeyman when I was at a very young age and even gave him a temporary identity, our old neighbour from the next farm, Mr. Pollychuck.

We had moved countless times over the ensuing years, and I would always arrive at our new home hoping that I had given the bogeyman the slip, but eventually I would dream about him again and wake up screaming to find his shadow slipping out of my bedroom.

I could never tell anyone about him; it was too embarrassing. I would cover up by just saying I was having a nightmare.

He continued to pay me occasional visits in my dreams well into my adulthood and continued to seem very real. It always took me several wide-awake minutes to clear my head and realize how ridiculous I was being.

Once, when I was in my early twenties, I woke up in a bed I shouldn't have been sharing, screaming and in a cold sweat. My companion was understandably startled, and when she asked me what the matter was I saved face and covered up by saying, "I thought I saw your husband coming into the room."

So, there it was: one minute I was the bold man in blue facing down incredible dangers and the next, when on the edge of sleep, jumping at shadows as the bogeyman followed me on my rounds.

At first I thought I would be able to soldier up and be immune to the temptation of snatching forty winks on the city's time, but that soon changed.

One night, as I made my way along a back alley behind Spadina Avenue with only some dog-sized Norwegian sewer rats for company, Morpheus swooped down out of a hazy city sky, wrapped his fuzzy wings

A dark alley off Spadina

around me and sapped my last ounce of resistance. I was so tired I couldn't move.

Opening one eye a slit, I noticed a flattened-out refrigerator box lying near the centre of the alley. It beckoned to me. A brand- new king sized Certa Perfect Sleeper complete with puffy duvet and satin pillows would not have been more inviting.

I couldn't help it. I staggered forward and collapsed on the cardboard, then, assuming a fetal position and holding my gun holster protectively with one hand and clutching my hat with its shiny badge like a teddy bear with the other, I drifted off to sleep. "And in that sleep of death what dreams shall come?"

I was dreaming that I was a child again and sleeping peacefully in the loft of our little house on the prairie. Then suddenly my dream turned into a familiar nightmare—that old bogeyman that had plagued me since early childhood had me pinned in a corner of the room and was blowing his cadaverous breath in my face.

I woke, screaming, to discover that the foul odour was real, but origin-ating from the toothless mouth of a grisly bum who was bending over me, checking to see if I was alive or dead. I suspect he was hoping for the latter, since as I awoke he quickly withdrew his hand from the vicinity of the pocket I kept my wallet in.

We never spoke, but before we parted company, with the sun rising into a smoggy sky, I tucked a two-dollar bill in his breast pocket, sort of hush money.

12: Bad Bob Dixon

I never met a man who hated being a policeman more than Robert Dixon. When I was a rookie in 52 Division I was often partnered up with him, and while we walked the beat or shared a squad car together he never stopped talking about how much he detested what he was doing and how he longed to be back home in England.

He was a strange guy, a man in his mid-thirties, a little taller than me but not overly large for a policeman. He was slim but solid-looking, scruffy, with swarthy hawk-like facial features topped with black hair, in a badly-executed brush cut. His uniform was littered with cigarette ashes, looking like the dog had slept on it. He had a general unwashed look about him and didn't seem to care. Even after several cautions from the Duty Sergeant he would turn up day after day flaunting a batterd old issue hat that he continued to wear even though he knew was against regulations.

While we were out on our first patrol together, he told me about the job he had left in the old country and how much he regretted his decision to immigrate. He said he had worked in the props department at Pinewood Movie Studios and went on to describe some of the films he had helped create sets for. He talked proudly of how he had learned how to make sheets of plywood and a few wooden dowels appear to be the riveted iron plates on the bridge of a battle-ship for a film about the naval battles in WWII, and other theatrical tricks he had learned.

I recognized a couple of the films he referred to, and if he was putting me on he was doing a good job of it. Most of my conversations with him centred on that part of his life, and I found it hard to believe the rumours I had heard about him.

Word was that he was very tough little scrapper who had grown up in the slums of London—quick with his fists and not afraid of anyone. Most of the guys on the job depended on their brawn for self-defence, but Bob was one of the few who had taken up the martial arts. He was always at me to join him at his Judo classes, but I never did. I adhered to my father's theory that it was a poor set of legs that let your nose get in trouble.

I got my first glimpse of the dark side of his personality one night when we were called to break up a bar fight at a local tavern. On our way into the place a big, aggressive-looking fellow waving a knife confronted us. While I was deciding whether to grab my nightstick or my gun, Bob casually reached into his pocket and pulled out a switchblade, then flicked the blade open inches from the man's nose. There was an evil glint in my partner's eyes as he stood staring the man down, and the effect was immediate. The man dropped his knife and stood transfixed while, after a nod from Bob, I cuffed him.

Bob's desire to be doing something other than police work had turned him into a rogue of sorts. He didn't care about the job anymore and was always up to the kind of stuff that could get most guys fired. I was spending a lot of time with him and although I liked the man, I was always worried that some of the things he dragged me into would result in both of us getting the boot. Small stuff like hiding from the patrol sergeant when he came to check on us, and then pelting him with snowballs.

He smoked in the scout cars, cadged free coffee from the restaurants, slept on the night shift, took the odd nip and never paid retail to any of the local merchants. These infractions were not that uncommon, but there were some other pretty serious breaches of conduct.

Thinking back, I suppose he was purposely trying to get the axe and for some reason wasn't very successful at it. His close relationship with some of the local hookers and bootleggers raised eyebrows, but even these transgressions didn't lead to his dismissal.

When I asked Maloney, another cop I was often partnered up with, why the department put up with Bob's shenanigans he shook his head and said, "The man was born with a horseshoe up his arse. He keeps pushing his luck with his dirty tricks but before they catch up with him, he usually comes up with a brilliant piece of police work that wipes his slate clean."

In the few weeks I had been working with Bob in 1964 he had pissed off so many of his superior officers and broken so many rules that I figured, despite what Maloney had said, it would be impossible for him ever to redeem himself.

I was wrong.

There had been a spate of bank robberies in the city. Montreal thugs were dropping by in droves to loot Toronto the Good.

The hold-up squad decided to call on the other ranks so they would have sufficient numbers to put plain-clothes officers posing as bank clerks in all the juicy targets like the banks on Yonge Street, and Bob and I drew the short straw.

It was bound to be a boring job. The only saving grace was that we didn't each need to spend a full shift at our assigned bank, the CIBC at 199 Yonge Street. I would do the first half of the day and, if Bob chose to show up on time, as he seldom did, he would handle the second.

We spent days at it walking around behind the counters, sweating in the tweed jackets we needed to wear to conceal our shoulder holsters. Bob was not one to hide his displeasure at being stuck in the bank, and when he wasn't complaining to the duty sergeant, he was moaning to the bank manager. I figured it was just a question of time 'til his bad attitude got him off the detail and, I hoped, me, too.

It didn't happen immediately, but one day, near the end of a long boring stretch, Bob came in to relieve me looking happy as hell. He told me that this was to be our last day in the banking business.

He was in such a good mood that he had uncharacteristically arrived an hour and a half before he needed to and didn't insist that I go and bring him back some coffee and doughnuts...a ritual on every other day.

I thanked him and told him that I was going to go directly to the station and arrange to use some of the time I had accumulated to have an afternoon off.

I was half- way home in my Volkswagen Beetle when I heard the news on my car radio. There had been an attempted robbery at our bank and an officer was wounded.

The rest of the story I got from the newspapers, and directly from Bob once he was out of the hospital. It seems that, shortly after I left him, Bob had retired to a secluded corner of the bank and lit up a smoke. He was wondering what the Department might have in store for him, now that he'd nagged his way out of this assignment, when he noticed something strange happening at one of the wickets.

Now this is when this story takes a turn that most people will be hesitant to believe, and if I hadn't recently found the pictures from the bank's security cameras to substantiate it, I would be hesitant to trust my own recollections. A burly goon in a trench coat and a fedora was confronting the lady teller behind the counter, and she wasn't looking at all happy. Bob reached inside his jacket and felt for his clumsy old issue Webley pistol and then flew into action. The man didn't see him approaching and Bob didn't see a weapon, so he decided to avail himself of some the techniques he had learned in his Judo classes and tried to wrestle the man down.

It turned out that the bull-necked robber was more monster than man, and he flung his two hundred and fifty pounds around, tossing Bob off like a fly. He landed in a heap, and that's when he saw the guy's gun.

Bob reached for his own revolver, but it was too late. The man fired, and the shot hit Bob in the lower abdomen, driving him down and sending his own gun skittering across the marble floor.

Seeing Bob writhing on the floor, the thug gathered up the cash he had stolen and, sneering in my fallen partner's direction, headed for the door, gun in hand.

Bob rolled over and reached down to his ankle, where, against all regulations, he had hidden a Beretta automatic pistol. He drew it and emptied its magazine into the guy's back.

The bandit died from his wounds but, believe it or not, Bob was *From the security camera* spared because the bullet he took hit him in his belt buckle.

If things had gone on schedule I would have been the guy in the bank when it was being robbed and the headlines might have read quite differently. "COP COWERS IN WASHROOM WHILE BANK IS ROBBED" or, God forbid, "ROOKIE POLICEMAN SHOT & KILLED"

Bob became an instant hero, receiving commendations and being lauded in the press. You would assume that he would finally be content with his lot in life.

Not so.

After he got out of the hospital he was given a promotion of sorts and was working with the detectives, but I heard through the grapevine that he was up to his old tricks again and had just about used up all the brownie points acquired by his exploits at the bank. He was at another low ebb when history repeated itself.

Bob and another detective answered a call for a robbery in progress at a liquor store on Davenport Road. As usual Bob, was the first man through the door and was confronted with a man with a gun. His own revolver was still holstered, so as he went for it he tried to bluff it out, telling the man to drop his weapon or he would shoot him.

"With what?" the man sneered, taking the opportunity to shoot Bob, driving him back against the door.

The robber then tried to dash past him but Bob, in spite of his wound, got his gun out and another crook bit the dust.

And so began another cycle. I don't know what became of him after he recovered from his second gunshot wound; I left the job shortly after and lost track.

Girl Teller Gives Alarm, P.C. Kills No. 1 Bandit

By TED STUEBING
Telegram Staff Reporter

A policeman took four chances with his life yesterday to protect bank customers before killing Toronto's number-one bank robber in a holdup on Yonge st.

Stunned and bleeding from a bullet graze on the side, Plainclothesman Robert Dixon, 37, took one shot to drop Gordon D. Peterson, 37, as he charged

GORDON D. PETERSON

Bank of Commerce at 199 Yonge st.

stantly. I didn't think I would, but I didn't have a moment's hesitation in pushing the alarm," she said.

Const. Dixon grabbed with Peterson and was hit by one of four shots fired at him by the gunman in his escape bid.

The policeman drew his gun but held back his fire until Peterson was between the two double doors at the bank entrance.

Then he fired and ran

Another Bob exploit

Years later, when I went to see the movie *Dirty Harry*, the people around me were seeing Clint Eastwood, but I was seeing my old friend Bob.

I have recently learned that Bob was belatedly awarded the Order of The British Empire (BEM) in 1968. He would be in his eighties by now, but I wouldn't be surprised to hear that he is still around. He was a hard bugger to kill.

13: Maybe I could be a detective

After Bad Bob Dixon brought down one of Canada's most infamous bank robbers in a gun battle in the bank on Yonge Street in 1964, I got it into my head that maybe I would like to be a detective. Okay, it was probably because of all the attention Bob was getting in the newspapers and on radio and TV. He had recently been placed in plain clothes in preparation to being moved up to official detective status.

I guess I was a bit jealous. We had both been in plain clothes in the bank and I had spent a lot of money on a nifty shoulder holster. I thought if I could make my mark and be noticed, I might also be considered; but as it turned out, opportunities for me to shine out of uniform were few and far between. I think it might have been due to my small stature and youthful appearance.

I thought I was on my way to my new goal when I got a call to report for duty in plain clothes. I was going to be sent to mingle in a crowd at a political rally in the ballroom at the Royal York Hotel.

Victor Copps of Hamilton was campaigning for the leadership of the Ontario Liberal Party. Apparently, these rallies at hotels could be danger-ous, as would be proven a few years later when Robert Kennedy was as-sassinated at the Ambassador Hotel in Los Angeles.

Nothing like that would be happening on my watch. I had been given the responsibility for all those involved, and I was sure I was up to the task. I took my time dressing in front of the mirror, practising my most intimidating looks while reaching under my suit jacket and whipping out my revolver.

I was ready and, after a quick word with the duty sergeant at the sta-tion, I headed to the hotel.

Things were already in full swing when I arrived in the lobby and ap-proached the ballroom entrance. I started to walk past two huge men in hotel uniforms—I think they were bouncers who were doubling as se-curity guards, but I was immediately halted by a thick arm thrust in front of my chest.

"Where do you think you're going, young fella? I don't see no invitation in your hand," the larger of the two barked.

With my best *how dare you* look, I said, "I'm a police officer, so would you kindly step aside."

"Yeah, sure, sonny. Why don't you piss off and go over to that cafeteria and buy yourself an ice cream cone?"

That did it—such disrespect! I whipped out my wallet and flashed the badge attached to it. "Read that and weep! Then get the hell out of my way. I've got a job to do."

Without removing his arm, he turned grinning to his partner and said, "Look here, another one of them badges out of the Cracker Jack boxes."

I leaned in close, opened my jacket and in desperation, whimpered, "Ah, come on boys. Give me a break. Check this out—a real gun and everything."

At that, they both began laughing hysterically and I panicked. I didn't know what to do. I couldn't call the station and tell them that they wouldn't let me in. So much for the beginning of my career as a detective.

I was almost in tears when I heard a familiar voice join in the laughter of the security guards. "Okay, dat's enough, boysDa joke's over. Turn da lidder fella loose before he does damage to ya."

What the hell was Maloney doing there, squeezed into a suit that looked like it was about to burst? I thought I was the only one assigned to the detail.

He came over and put his arm around over my shoulder and said, "I heard you was comin' and I just wanted a bit of fun."

"Yeah, at my expense, you miserable big bastard."

"Now don't be like dat, sonny. When we gets done here I'll take you over to the restaurant and assault you wid a steak and see if we can get some meat on those skinny bones of yours. I knows the chef—he'll treat us right."

Thus ended my aspirations of becoming another Joe Friday of *Dragnet* fame.

14: Good Cop Bad Cop

I was standing on a corner a stone's throw from old 57 Division Station, holding my memo book open and watching the evening traffic go, by recording RMNIs.

Rear Marker Not Illuminated, or RMNI, was a traffic offence that didn't require a policeman to stop and confront the driver and, more importantly for me, it was counted as an infraction and was recorded on the cop's record. But just a warning letter was sent out in place of a summons, so no harm was done and the quota system, that the department denied existed, was appeased.

I hated giving out parking tickets and charging people with moving offences so, until the department took a closer look at my score sheet, this would have them fooled.

When a big old Cadillac with an unlit, mud-coated licence plate stopped at the curb in front of the Greek restaurant across from the station and a man got out and headed into it, I decided that it would be a good opportunity to circumvent the system and give the man a friendly personal caution. I waited until he came back out, coffee and sandwich in hand, then hailed him over to the rear of his car.

That's when I noticed the row of what appeared to bullet holes in the trunk lid.

My rapidly developing cop sense of when something was wrong kicked in, so, pretending not to notice the holes, I asked to see his licence and insurance certificate.

When he said he had left them at home, I suggested that he come across the street to the station, saying, "It'll only take a moment and you can eat your sandwich while I confirm that your licence is valid. I'm sure everything will be alright."

He seemed reluctant, but when I casually started brushing at the leather of my gun holster, he said, "Yeah, yeah, okay, Let's get this over with. I'm in a hurry."

When we got to the station, I tried to introduce him to the desk sergeant. "This is Mister...sorry, sir. What did you say your name is?"

The man looked around the locked room we were in and, seemingly resigned to his fate, said, "I didn't say and I'm not going to say. If I'm not under arrest you have to let me go about my business."

"Now, don't get upset, my friend," the sergeant said. "You just sit tight here for a bit and I'll have a word with the young constable here and we'll sort this out."

When we were alone, and I told the sergeant about what I thought were bullet holes in the back of the man's car, he said, "You keep an eye on him. He can't get out and I feel like a coffee. I think I'll go over to the restaurant. I might glance at the mystery man's vehicle as I go by."

When he came back, no coffee in hand, he said, "Let's take our friend upstairs to the interrogation room. Those are bullet holes, alright. I'd say 45 calibre. He's got some explaining to do. I'll call the holdup squad to give us a visit. You can see if you can get anything out of him yourself. It might take a while for them to get here."

I immediately thought, *This is my opportunity, my big chance to hone my detective skills.* I had seen it all in the movies: the good cop, bad cop ploy.

To make my plan work I would need another constable to assist me, but when I asked the sergeant for help, he said the only other person available was a policewoman.

I knew Gerta. We had been at the police college together, so, reluctantly, I decided to include her in my plan.

She was a stocky, full-bodied woman, a German immigrant who maintained a bit of an accent. She was a brusque, no-nonsense type who, when I observed her filling in for the matron in the women's cells, gave the place a kind of terrifying prison vibe.

"So, Gerta, you understand the way it works: a tough mean cop tries to scare the information out of the subject, and when he's out of the room, a sympathetic good cop apologizes for the behaviour of the bad cop hoping to win his confidence and get him to spill the beans."

"Okay, Garry, I'll be the bad cop."

"No, Gerta, I'm sorry, I have to be the bad cop. You can't be the bad cop."

"Vy not?"

"Because you're a woman and women don't appear tough and threatening enough."

"I'm probably tougher and more threatening than you, you twerp.

65

Let's arm-wrestle to see who gets to be the bad guy."

I was moderately sure that I could beat her but, being careful I decided that a coin-toss would be more appropriate. I won and then explained what we would be doing, confident that I would have our prisoner confessing in no time at all.

What ensued over the following hour was a series of short, chaotic dramas performed for an audience of one bored, unimpressed felon. Periodically I would storm into the room demanding information, bellowing threats, slamming my fist onto the desk, wagging my night stick and kicking chairs over until Gerta dragged me out of the room and started schmoozing him herself.

It was all to no avail until, during the last of my attempts, the room fell silent and the light that had been coming through the entrance door went dark and long shadow made its way over to where we were.

A huge man, built like a refrigerator, wearing a trench coat and a fedora, removed a cigar and stepped slowly in, ignoring Gerta and me, and addressed our prisoner.

"We meet again, Curly," he uttered in a throaty growl, then nodded a get-lost signal in our direction.

Thirty minutes later the gargantuan detective came down to where Gerta and I waited and handed me a large manila envelope.

"We're taking your prisoner down to 52 Division. This is his confession. Don't look so disappointed, sonny, you'll get the hang of it."

But I knew I never would. Gerta had been right. I had been acting like a *dummkopf*. She would have made a better bad cop.

One reason the detective commanded so much respect was that he was close to seven feet tall and weighed over three hundred pounds. I decided there and then that the only way I could ever hope to approach or better that kind of image was to give in and join the Mounted Unit. Seated on a saddle, I would instantly become ten feet tall, with over twelve hundred pounds of prancing horseflesh to back me up.

So that's what I did.

15: Ghost story

When I was working the midnight shift, there was one spot on a beat that I dreaded covering. The stores and office buildings on the southwest corner of Young and St. Clair streets conceal the sprawling old St. Michael's Cemetery, and it was part of my job to make sure that the rear entrances to those stores were safe and secure. This meant that I would have to venture into the dark back lane that separated them from the graveyard.

On the best of nights this was one eerie place to be, but on the night in question it was even more intimidating, with a full moon reflecting off the shiny tombstones and mausoleums and making it look like a set from a Boris Karloff movie. My first instinct was to turn around, leave and fudge my memo book to make it look like I had been there.

But I couldn't do that, so, instead, I took a deep breath and pressed on.

I rounded the corner and started testing door handles, trying not to spend too much time looking at the graveyard. By the time I reached the far end of the block, my teeth had stopped chattering, and my knees were a little less wobbly.

When I turned around to head back down the alley and the full panorama of the graveyard swung into view again, I saw something that stopped me in my tracks.

A white, gossamer-clad apparition appeared in the moonlight, dancing from headstone to headstone, trailing a long white veil behind her.

It's true that in moments of terror your hair does really stand on end and, with the amount of anxious energy that was flowing up through my follicles, I'm surprised that that my hat didn't fly off.

At first I wasn't able to move, but then I heard a voice in the back of my head say, "Legs don't fail me now!" and they didn't. I ran like a scalded cat down the lane and into the bright lights of Young Street.

As I stood catching my breath and trying to make sense of what had just happened, I realized that I had only two choices. I could go back into that lane and face whatever waited for me, or I could go back to the station, turn in my badge and gun, and hop a streetcar down to 999 Queen Street W., Toronto's renowned mental institution.

Somehow, I gathered the courage. Convinced that my life as I knew it, was probably over, I started the return journey towards the graveyard.

I was hoping that it all had been my imagination, and as I approached the spiked, wrought-iron fence that enclosed the cemetery, my theory seemed to be holding true. There was no one and no thing to be seen.

I'd forced myself to come that far, so what the hell, why not walk a short way into the graveyard and bolster my recovering self-esteem even further?

Stepping more confidently now, I made my way through the tombstones toward a huge marble monument that towered over the other memorials. As I reached its far side, I saw something that made me gasp so violently that I almost swallowed my tongue.

There, reclining on the base of the monument, was my ghost.

My head said run but my legs wouldn't obey. I just stood anchored to the ground. I tried to close my eyes and blink her away, but she remained, and so close I could have reached out and touched her.

As I watched, she seemed to levitate to her feet then float towards me with an outstretched arm.

My feet refused to move so I closed my eyes and arched my head and body backwards as far as I could.

It wasn't the cold and clammy claw I anticipated. Instead, I felt a soft warm hand caressing my arm and as I came out of my terror-induced paralysis I realized that I was confronting a real, live woman and she was asking me if I was all right and seemed really concerned.

After escorting me back to a rear door that led to her apartment above one of the stores and reviving me with a coffee laced with brandy, she explained that she was an interpretative dancer and that she often practised her routines in the graveyard at night.

After a second brandy I thanked my ghostly Isadora Duncan for her hospitality and sheepishly took my leave.

16: An outing to Aurora

I had only been a policeman for a couple of months when one morning, instead of parading for duty at our station as we usually did, a group of us, all new recruits, were told to grab our lunches and board a dark-green bus with military markings.

Most of us were recently out of high school, so it felt like the beginning of a class outing. We all sat chatting cheerfully away, wondering where we were going, as the bus made a couple of turns then headed north on Toronto's central Yonge Street.

But, when our bus came to a halt further north, near Willowdale, our mood changed abruptly. The doors at the front of the bus flew open and our divisional Inspector and an Army officer climbed aboard.

"Button up and listen to this man. He has something very important to tell you," the Inspector shouted.

The army officer, who was dressed in camouflage fatigues, began, "Gentlemen, we are all going to head further north to a very special place. Only a very few privileged people know about it. It's been a complete secret until recently and, after today, you will also be charged with keeping that secret. Now, will you all pull down those curtains on the windows beside you and remain silent."

The two officers took their seats and we moved off. I had no idea where we might be going. I didn't hear or feel the bus turning, so I assumed we were continuing northward.

About a half an hour later, when the bus came to halt, the Inspector spoke to us in a stern, hushed voice. "Grab your lunches, keep your traps shut and follow me!"

I stepped out, last in line, into the blinding sunlight. We had pulled in close to an ordinary-looking farmhouse resting in a sizable pasture.

The Inspector ordered us into single file and directed us into the back door of the house. Once we were inside, we were hurried over to the entrance of a concealed passageway.

As a group we carefully snaked our way down a long, dark stairwell into an equally dark area at the bottom. We heard the doors above us slam shut then the area burst into light.

We were in a huge, long, high-ceilinged, tube like, echoing concrete vault with chalk boards, maps and detailed signage mounted around the walls. It was reminiscent of the set of *Dr. Strangelove*.

"Find a chair and settle in. You all looked confused," the Army officer said in a comforting tone. He had hurried ahead and placed himself behind a lectern at the front of the room.

"I'll explain. This is a special bunker built to protect certain members of the government and other essential people in event of a nuclear attack. Some people have called this, and other ones like it around the country, Diefenbunkers, but it's nothing to joke about and you policemen will have a very important role in making it successful. You've all been around long enough to know that it's possible that someday five hundred EMO sirens will start wailing across Canada to announce an imminent nuclear attack. This place would be of no use if the people with the skills to guide us through it couldn't get here in a timely fashion. That's where you guys come in."

We all looked around at each other, puffed up with self-importance but curious as to what important role we would be playing. We were all good-looking young men so my immediate thought was that maybe they would want to use us as poster boys for an awareness campaign.

Or maybe it was the kids they were thinking of. Maybe they were considering adding us to the Elmer The Safety Elephant school project. Look both ways before crossing a road and duck and cover when the sirens start.

I was trying to imagine what Elmer would look like with a gas mask on when my revelry was interrupted.

"In order to move traffic out of the city quickly," he continued, "particularly in a panicked situation with the likelihood of a power failure affecting the traffic lights at the intersections, we will need policemen at those locations to direct traffic A great deal of planning and scheduling has already been done and you people are the remaining few who haven't been assigned their intersection. But no fear: I have your assignments here."

"Have no fear?" I gulped inaudibly.

The officer reached into a briefcase and lifted out a pile of memo-sized yellow papers and handed them to the inspector. "Sir, would you please hand these to the appropriate constables. The names and badge numbers are at the top."

The inspector called out our names and, one by one, we came forward to receive the bad news. Yonge and Eglington: two street names that I would never forget were printed in capital letters on my copy.

I couldn't believe it. Did they really believe that one day we, alerted by the moaning of the air raid sirens, would pull out our traffic direction kits, don our white conducting gloves, test our whistles, and head out to a certain death trying to help save a doomed fleeing population?

But wait a minute. It hit me. *There's a hell of a lot of people in Toronto.*

So I ventured a question. "Excuse me, sir, but could you tell me how many people would fit in here?"

"Lots, constable, lots," he shot back.

Another constable raised his hand. "Could you be more specific, sir?"

The officer looked a little miffed. "Just read those damned signs on the walls. They've got all the details."

We left our seats and began milling around the huge room.

One officer whispered, "Read it and weep boys. I don't like the looks of this."

One chalk board had spaces to record the casualties in the area, dead and wounded and those to be rescued. Another was there to record radiation data, dosage rates and exposures.

I guesstimated the number of policemen and women that it would take to cover all those intersections and had to force myself not to pick up the piece of chalk that lay close to the board and scratch the number in the space for confirmed dead. If I had had the courage, I would have finished with the chalk, turned to the two officers and said, "Just saving everybody a little time. When the time comes, if it ever does, you can be sure of this many at least."

But of course, I didn't. Instead, when one of the other constables pointed out an escape hatch that led to a storage shed outside, I found myself considering using it to escape the situation...tossing my cap and uniform aside and running southward down to the city to turn in my warrant card and gun and resign.

Another sign suggested that there were 100 phone lines installed. Could that also be the maximum number of people who would be offered shelter? It wasn't fair, and I didn't want any part of it.

As a kid during the Cold War, when I was in public school, I was always the class leader waiting until the other kids were all safely down under their desks in the duck and cover drills before I got under mine. I was repeatedly devising bomb shelters from discarded bits of lumber and old beds in the basements of the various houses we moved to after the hydrogen bomb threat reared its evil head, and was always offering to share them with anyone who wanted to join me.

Later in my late teens, when the Cuban Missile Crisis was at its climax and about to destroy us all, I took shelter under a kitchen table that I willingly shared with several others at an End of the World party.

Now this...There was no justice in the world. this was going too damned far. Did they really expect me to leave my loved ones behind and go and stand at an intersection to be toasted to charcoal while a few dignitaries got to slip up here to safety?

As tempted as I was to voice an immediate protest, a burst of caution muzzled me. There was no way anybody really would, or could, have done what they were requiring of us, but I was not going to be the only one to point that out, not that day.

I hear that the old bunker in Aurora is just a tourist attraction now, a testament to the futility of planning for an elite, seemingly more important, sector of society to survive a nuclear holocaust. No intelligent person would believe that the effects of a five-megaton atomic bomb would be survivable, and countless men in blue uniforms would have been among the first to be killed.

Now over fifty years later, as I stare at the faded yellow memo sheet that I found in an old wallet of mine, I can only wonder at how lucky we all have been to survive, and continue to survive, despite the constant, unending threats we live under.

17: Officer down!

Maloney and I were teamed up in a scout car, patrolling out of 52 Division, when our radio lit up and we received an urgent call.

"Officer down!" "Officer down!" the anxious sounding dispatcher repeated. "Any unit in the vicinity of Bloor and Bathurst please report."

Maloney picked up the microphone; pressed the speak button and drawled, "Scout 523 we're near scene."

The dispatcher immediately replied, "523 proceed as fast as you can to the corner of Shaw and Barton. A woman is reporting that a mounted policeman has fallen off his horse and is lying unconscious on her front lawn. She thinks he has had a heart attack."

I pushed the siren button and hit the accelerator and in matter of minutes we arrived at the scene.

I saw the horse first, he was busy grazing on the lawn and flower beds in front of the house. And there, almost under him, lay a very still policeman.

I threw my car door open, and as I was about to leap out I noticed that Maloney once again had the microphone in his hand.

"Dispatcher this is Scout 523. We're at the scene, cancel all other units. We'll handle this," he said.

He seemed unusually calm about what seemed to be a very serious situation.

I hurried over to the house, where a woman who was obviously very upset stood on her doorstep nervously twisting her apron. "He's dead, I know he's dead," she kept repeating.

I started toward the downed cop, but I felt Maloney's big hand on shoulder. He pushed by me and knelt beside the prostrate figure.

The man on the ground was an older-looking policeman in dirty breeches and scruffy riding boots; his hair was long and matted and it had been a while since his face had seen a razor.

Maloney felt for the man's pulse and leaned in closer to smell his

73

breath. "Phew," he whispered. He's dead all right, dead drunk."

Then he turned toward the woman on the porch and announced in a loud voice, "You were quite right, Madame, this constable has had a heart attack, but he is still alive. In cases like this," he continued, "time is of the essence, so we better take him to the hospital in our patrol car. If we wait for an ambulance, it might be too late."

With that, he unceremoniously scooped the old guy up and, while I held the door open, threw him into the back seat of our scout car.

"The stables ain't far away," he said. "I'll take him there. Do you think you can lead that nag that far without getting trampled?"

"I'll try," I said.

I made my way over to the big gelding and watched with pleasure the look of astonishment on Maloney's face as he watched me grab the reins, vault into the saddle and take off down the street ahead of him.

I took a short cut through Christie Pits park and, putting the horse into a canter, beat Maloney to the stables on London Street. I had just put the horse into a vacant stall when he came through the door with the very limp cop cradled in his arms.

"Climb up that loft ladder and I'll pass him up to you," he said.

I made my way up, dragged the drunk through the loft hole, then made him comfortable on a pile of loose hay and left him to sleep it off.

As I descended the ladder, I heard Maloney on the phone, arranging for somebody to come and take the guy home.

"So, you're quite the cowboy," Maloney joked as we drove away. "Why don't you join the mounted unit?"

"That guy up in the loft is the reason I'm not interested," I replied. "I've heard that half the guys in the unit are losers like him. Besides, I'm hav-ing a lot of fun doing what I'm doing."

I explained to Maloney that I had been messing around with horses for as long as I could remember. I told him how I had spent my summers breaking and training horses and ponies for the summer camps and about the little riding school I ran while attending high school.

'I have two horses of my own at my parents' farm in Meaford, and I'm up there every time I get a day off," I said. "Hell, I get all the riding I need as it is."

18: Meeting The Man

Mounted Unit headquarters

Several weeks later, when I got a call to report to mounted headquarters for a meeting with Inspector Johnson, I figured that Maloney had let the cat out of the bag and that I was about to be recruited. I didn't know how I was going to explain to the man in charge why I didn't want to have anything to do with the unit, without insulting him. I was determined to resist any sunshine he was about to blow up my ass concerning what a glorious future I might look forward to, fighting crime on horseback.

As it turned out, I didn't have a chance to say anything. Inspector Johnson, or Big Ed, as the boys in his unit affectionately called him, broke right into his spiel. Tapping his finger on a pile of papers on his desk he asked me, "Do you know what this is, Leeson?"

I confided that I didn't.

"Well, let me tell you what this is," he said, slamming his fist down on the desk. "This is about the most important God-dammed thing that has ever happened around here!"

I'll admit he had sparked my curiosity.

Picking up the papers and fanning them in my direction he said, "What I have in my hand is the final authorization for the expansion of the mounted unit. We're going to fill all those old stables again. Hell, they've even agreed to build some new ones. Imagine," he said, "forty or fifty new horses and twice that many men.

He finally took a breath, and I used the opportunity to formulate an intelligent question. "Howcum?" I blurted out.

"Howcum?" he roared, "I'll tell you howcum, The bastards have finally realized just how valuable mounted units are, Don't you read the papers, son? There's riots breaking out all over the world and what's the best way to deal with them? Horses, horses and more horses."

He got to his feet and paced up and down the width of his office as he railed on about the advantages of using horses for police work, and only stopped when another inspector with some urgent business to attend to appeared in his open doorway.

I felt like I had been to revival meeting as I accepted his card and took my leave.

"Call me, son," he said. "I need men like you."

As good as his sermon was, I had not yet seen the light and dismissed the idea of joining up.

19: Ron does it again

Some weeks later I broached the idea with my friend and now fellow constable Ron Bond.

"Are you out of your mind?" he said. "How could you even consider joining those smelly buggers? They all constantly smell of horse shit. It's embarrassing, the rest of us won't sit anywhere near them in court, and when they get on streetcars people get off. Get with it, man, this is 1964. We're about to try a lunar landing and you want to spend your time riding those stinking beast's around!"

As usual, he was fairly convincing, so I finished my beer and left it at that. Anyway, I had other fish to fry.

Because I was always sketching and drawing cartoons, and they sometimes got copied and passed around, I had an offer to become apprenticed to Detective Sergeant Magurie, who did all the composite drawings for the department. I had been given lots of time to think the offer over, and after six weeks of pondering I had just about made up my mind to add an artist's beret to my uniform.

That's when I received an order to report to mounted headquarters once again. I showed up out of uniform and looking weekend shabby in a T-shirt and jeans I wasn't trying to impress anyone; in fact, I was hoping for the opposite effect.

I was shown into the inspector's office by the desk sergeant. and Big Ed immediately got to his feet and grabbed my hand. "Welcome aboard, Leeson, I'm glad you decided to join up."

I was flabbergasted and almost floored, so I shot back at him in language I knew he would understand. "Whoa! Steady! Easy! I haven't said that I was joining up."

"What do you mean?" the inspector said. "Your buddy said you were ready to start right away."

"Buddy? What buddy?" I said.

"Constable Ronald Bond" he replied. "He's been training with the riding school for the last three weeks; there's only one week left to go, and we had one man flunk out. He said you didn't really need any training and could jump right in and replace him. Is there a problem?"

I was speechless, but I knew when I was licked. *What the hell*, I thought.

Then I turned to the inspector and said, "Where are my spurs?"

Inspector 'Big Ed' Johnson

20: Festival Italiano

I suppose every kid has dreams of running away and joining a circus, and in 1967 I almost did. I was spending a lot of time breaking and training remounts in the Horse Palace at the exhibition grounds in Toronto; it was a dark, dreary, tomb of a place when the C.N.E. or The Royal Winter Fair weren't in session.

One day, when I showed up for work expecting more of the same, I was greeted instead with a bright and wonderful surprise. My gloomy old cave of a workplace had somehow been transformed into a magical, glittering cavern. The long aisles, normally dark, were fully illuminated, and hundreds of brightly coloured costumes hung from rows of clothing racks on either side of the alleyway. There were strange looking props and equipment, full suits of medieval armour, spears, swords, shields, jousting sticks and piles and piles of unidentifiable paraphernalia.

Parked in the open area at the centre of the building were two beautiful golden chariots; on the walls beside each them hung four sets of the most incredibly ornate, jewel-encrusted harnesses. About fifty newly-arrived horses occupied the stalls.

When I got to the police stables, I found Inspector Johnson and Sergeant Peddlar in conversation with two men, who I later learned were executives from MGM, the movie studio. That was when I learned what was going on.

A production called *Festival Italiano* that was due to tour the U.S. was going to be rehearsed and given a pre-tour opening in the Coliseum next door to the building in which we stood; the huge cast and the large number of props and costumes involved had made it necessary for them to spill over into the stable area and use it for storage and a large dressing room, as well as housing their many horses.

Because it was a last-minute decision, nobody had informed the Police Department, and the Inspector and sergeant weren't all that comfortable with the decision.

"We're training men and horses in the riding ring right in the center of all that hoopla," the Inspector said, "and we have deadlines to meet. We can't stop or move now!"

The guy from MGM assured him that they would not in any way interfere with what we were up to. The conversation went back and forth several time before a compromise was made: if the production company agreed to have their people stay out of our riding ring and leave a gap in the dressing room tables that surrounded one end of the enclosure, so that I could get my horses and students in and out, then things would be all right.

Things started out rather well. Merle Smith, the other trainer I worked with, got two young horses into the ring and we started teaching them to neck rein.

From where we sat, high on our horses' backs, we could see the ballerinas begin to arrive from their rooms at the Royal York Hotel. There were about thirty of them and not a homely one in the batch, although Merle suggested that some of them might have conformation problems when he saw the way they walked with their feet at strange angles.

The stunt men, who also looked after the show's horses, had just arrived from California were busy checking and grooming their animals, but Merle and I were a lot more interested in what was going on in the dressing room area.

There was nothing shy about those Italian girls, and although we initially tried to avert our eyes, the scene was so continuous and pervasive we finally relaxed and enjoyed the scenery. How did the saying go? 'When in Rome, or Toronto as the case may be do as the Romans do'.

All and all, it was a marvellous first day and for the first time in months I was looking forward to coming to work the next day.

When I arrived for work the following morning, things had already ramped up and rehearsals had begun in earnest. The teams of four-abreast horses were hooked into the chariots and were practising racing in the main arena. What a spectacular sight they were as they flew, hell bent for leather, around the arena, kicking up tanbark dust. They were the same chariots that had been used in the movie *Ben Hur*; no cheap theatrical mock-ups, the real thing.

The event that I was most interested in preceded the finale but was equally exciting; a jousting court was set up with a contraption that the knights of old used to improve their skills. It consisted of the torso of a dummy knight in armour suspended on a pivoting post; on the end of one extended arm was a shield and at the end of the opposing arm was a mace on the end of a short chain. The challenge for the mounted knight was to charge the device at a full gallop with his lance engaged and strike the shield. Of course, the impact would cause the dummy to instantly pivot and swing the mace at the knight; he had to be really quick and agile to avoid it.

Of course, the studded ball on the end of the chain that was traditionally made of cast iron was now made of foam rubber, but the thing could still give you a hell of a whack if you weren't careful. That's what happened one day as I spent my lunch hour watching a practice. One of the stunt men was swept from his horse and landed in a clattering heap on the ground.

The crew got him up and out of his armour and off to the hospital. Although he wasn't seriously hurt, it was clear that he wouldn't be getting back on his horse for a few days, and there was nobody to replace him.

This posed a real problem for the producer, because he had a dress rehearsal coming up shortly and some of his backers were flying in from California to check out the show, so he surprised me by asking if I thought I could stand in for the injured man.

I was dying to give the jousting a try anyway, but it wasn't all that simple for me. Technically I would be moonlighting, and although I knew most of the brass on the mounted unit would turn a blind eye, I wasn't so sure about Sergeant Pedlar. For some reason he had been giving me a real hard time lately. I hadn't given him any reason but seemed he not to trust me and was constantly riding me.

Sgt. Pedlar with his favourite horse, Duchess.

But the lure was too strong, so I decided to throw caution to the winds and accepted the offer. I spent a couple of evenings and early mornings practising and, after getting a couple of hard slaps on the back, seemed to get the hang of it.

The rest of the cast members were starting to treat me like one of their own. The ballerinas would spend a lot of time watching me when I was on duty, training the police horses or conducting riding classes; one in particular was constantly bugging me to let her ride one of our horses and, although I explained that it was strictly against regulations, she persisted day after day till finally, in a moment of weakness, I succumbed to the way she pleaded in her cute, lisping broken English and gave her a leg up onto old Roy, tutu and all.

I gave her a few elementary instructions and hoped that she would be satisfied, but she was back the next day looking for more. This time she had three more of the girls with her and they were anxious to join the class. Well fair is fair! I didn't want to show favouritism, somebody might get the wrong idea. Besides, we had several older horses in the stable who hadn't been getting much exercise lately.

Emboldened by the fact that Sergeant Pedlar hadn't been around hassling me lately, I decided to take a chance and increase the size of my class. I knew there would be hell to pay if the sergeant ever caught me, but as I watched those beautiful women bouncing around the ring in their tights, leg warmers, and braless bikini tops, it seemed well worth the risk.

The girls were quick learners, and before the week was out they were trotting and cantering around the ring like real pros.

At the beginning of the following week, midway through our, now-regular class I caught a glimpse of something that made my blood run cold: in a darkened corner outside the ring stood Sergeant Pedlar, leering in my direction.

That's it, the jigs up, I've had it, and my career is over!

I pretended not to see him as he opened the gate and started walking over to where I waited in the centre of the ring. I was not going to demean myself in front of my ladies. He might be able to take my job away from me, but I was keeping my dignity.

I could hear him breathing over my shoulder as he stood behind me, watching the ballerinas circle around us at a sitting trot. When he finally opened his mouth and started to speak I was ready for the worst.

Instead, he simply pointed in the direction of the class and said, "Tell the one with the big tits to keep her heels down!"

Then he turned and walked away without a further word.

The days of magic lasted for about two weeks more, and I gradually became more involved with the production, occasionally filling in for the charioteers and knights at the performances, I was also included in all the cast parties and informal gatherings, and it was during one of these that the producer asked me to join the show. He assured me that the money would be good and that when the tour ended in Los Angeles he would find me a permanent job with one of the studios.

I actually considered the offer for a matter of minutes; then reality set in and I knew I had too many responsibilities where I was for it to be a real possibility.

I enjoyed every remaining precious minute of my time with the show, and when I had to say goodbye and watch the long line of buses and trucks turn out of the exhibition grounds and head on their way to New York, the street sign said, 'The Queensway West', but for me it was 'The road not taken'!

21: The Horse Palace

It felt like the end of summer camp as I watched the last of my trainees stagger, stiff and bow-legged, out the door and on to their new postings. I knew it would be quite a while before I would see another class, and until then it would just be me and Merle, the other horse trainer, in that big, old building.

Working with young horses can be very interesting and rewarding, but as day after monotonous day passed by in that dark, old structure and now without the frequent presence of the Inspector, my greatest detractor and nemesis, Sergeant Peddlar, had a free hand to heap me with his unwarranted criticisms. He always, seemed to be looking over my shoulder and waiting for any excuse to discredit me.

The other guys would tell me that the sergeant had a sick sense of humour and was just turning my crank, and that beneath his crusty exterior he was a fun-loving guy. I couldn't believe that they were talking about the same man. I began to yearn for a transfer to someplace outdoors and away from the cranky sergeant.

The Horse Palace is a huge, two-story stable located in the Canadian National Exhibition grounds in Toronto. It's only used to its full capacity on two or three occasions during the year, notably the exhibition and the winter fair. During those times it houses hundreds of show horses and is crammed with thousands of competitors and admirers. During the rest of the year the building becomes a dark, dank, echoing vault with only two areas of the building in use and illuminated.

One corner of the stables had been partitioned off and allocated to the police horses in training and, nearby, diffused sunlight shone through a dirty skylight and down onto a riding ring near the centre of the building. During their training in the building, the young remounts must have felt more like pit ponies than police horses.

It was to this building that I was forced to drag myself day after monotonous day.

22: The Junkman's horse

When I was a teenager in Toronto, in addition to the saddle horses on the police mounted unit, there were still a few delivery horses plodding through the streets and alleys of the inner city. I knew almost all of them them and lots of their names.

There were the big, well-groomed greys in polished harness hitched to Borden's Dairy delivery wagons. Or the snappy little two-horse teams pulling Silverwood's Dairy rigs. The bakeries were still providing horse-drawn door-to-door service and all the various companies competed to have the best turned-out equipment and animals to represent them.

But it was not all slick animals and polished brass with bulging feed-bags. There were still a couple of low-budget operations whose horses and wagons reflected their limited resources. In contrast to the modern company delivery vans of the bread and dairy companies that boasted modern, easy turning wheels with pneumatic rubber tires, were the few, ancient, rattletrap, iron-shod wagons favoured by those in the junk trade.

We called them Ragmen, but they were often called worse names. The lack of respect for some of these hard-working men was, for the most part, because of the way they treated their horses. Often single, skinny, undersized animals in harness held together with twine and bailing wire pulling loads out of proportion to their size and strength.

It was my hope that, since the number of horses in the city was gradu-ally dwindling that soon the sound of hoofbeats on the tarmac would dis-appear altogether, and that, mercifully, these poor, mistreated, over-worked nags would be the first, one way or another, to find some rest.

But that's not the way it turned out.

Years later, by the time I joined the police force and ended up on the mounted unit, all the company horses in the city had been made redund-ant and sent out to pasture. But there was one notable exception.

If the Ragman's horse was a five-year-old when I first noticed him, he must have been in his twenties when he assumed the title of the last draft horse in Toronto.

It was nothing to celebrate. It was embarrassing and, as most people said, keeping the animal working was a damned crime. Eventually it did amount to a crime.

One day, one of my fellow mounted constables came riding into our stable yard on his horse, slow-stepping to accommodate Junkman's horse which was following, lame and limping, on a long lead.

"Take the poor bugger into the stable. There's an extra empty stall. I've got to go in and call the humane society," he called to me.

The Junkman was charged and an immediate court order took the matter out of our hands. A van showed up and took the horse away, and for a long time that was the last I saw or heard anything about him.

I had been off the police force for a couple of years when somebody told me that they had met a woman who, years earlier, had heard about the plight of the Junkman's horse and had arranged through the courts and the Humane Society to get custody of the old gelding, and was still providing a home for him.

Margo Colpitts was a single, fiftyish woman who lived with a menagerie of rescued animals on a small rented farm on the outskirts of the city. "C'mon up anytime she shouted into the phone!" after I told her who I was and why I was calling.

I could hear loud clucking in the background and the sound of a scuffle as she slammed the receiver down.

Andrea, my wife, decided to come with me when I headed up to see her.

When we pulled into her yard, two goats and a miniature pig jumped up from a shady spot, formed a greeting party, and stayed close to us as we approached the back door of the red brick farmhouse.

Margo saw us coming and, as we arrive on the porch, she opened the door just enough to get us in, then, with a barrage of expletives that would have made a sailor blush, sent the nosy animals who had accompanied us on their way.

"C'mon in and set down. I just put the kettle on." She indicated a couple of chairs at a huge formal dining table pressed close to an open door that was positioned close what appeared to be a woodshed.

After she shooed away a flapping rooster who had been occupying our seats, she pointed to the surface of the table that was totally filled, a foot high, with antique dishes and cutlery. "I'm a collector," she explained.

There was no doubt about that, and it appeared that it wasn't just dishes and furniture. She had just begun to tell me about the Junkman's horse when the head and shoulders of a Jersey cow thrust its way through a back door, hitting the edge of the table and sending several dishes flying and crashing to the floor.

"Now, that's going too god damned far! Get the hell out of there."

It took considerable time to chase the cow out of the kitchen and back to her pasture, but finally Margo was able to resume her story.

"You won't believe how much money and time I have spent on that old bastard. Vet bills, special feed, and god knows what."

"What's his name?" Andrea asked

"The old bugger who owned him showed up here one day looking for him. Said his name was Isak. I think he wanted him back, but there was no way. When I told him that I was having trouble feeding him, he just laughed.

"'Isak will eat anything,' he said. 'He's lived on stale bread and rotten fruit and vegetables and a smidgeon of hay for the ten years I've owned him.'

"That's when I showed him the door," Margo said with an evil look on her face. "It's been keeping me poor, but I give him all the bread, fruit and vegetables I can lay my hands on, and he seems fat and happy now. The vet says that this kind of diet shouldn't work and might be dangerous. C'mon out and look at him. Let me know what you think."

We walked out to the edge of the paddock, me expecting to see the skeletal bag of bones I remembered. Under the shade of a big elm a small, thickset bay gelding with a glossy coat had his muzzle deep in the sweet grass beside a low bin filled with day-old bread, fruit and vegetables.

No, bread is not particularly healthy for horses. They can easily digest all the basic ingredients used in bread, such as salt, yeast, flour, and water. Thus, there's nothing about bread that is specifically toxic or unhealthy to a horse, and the high-calorie content in bread, in fact, helps young horses in gaining weight. However, the problem lies with the absence of any significant nutritional value in bread.

That's the science of it. For this particular horse, though, Margo seemed to be feeding him the bread of life.

23: Lightbulb

It would be misleading to suggest that all policemen were either big, kind, sensitive hulks like Maloney or young, bumbling aspirants like myself. Every profession has its share of good and bad guys, and the police force is no different. I met many colourful rogues who bucked the system but were still tolerable to work with, but there were others who were simply mean, no-good bastards.

One such man in the latter category was Lightbulb Smith. I don't know how he got the name; he was already a fixture in the mounted unit when I started.

Will Rogers is quoted as saying, "I never met a man I didn't like." He had not met Lightbulb.

I think he had been forced to join the mounted unit when he lost his license after being convicted for drunken driving. That's what I heard, and the story seemed consistent with my observations of his behaviour. There was more than one occasion when I was enlisted to help hoist him into the loft to sleep one off when he was too drunk to drive home.

Once, playing the Good Samaritan, I bundled him into the back seat of my car and drove him to his home, only to have his distraught wife refuse to take him in. On our return to the stable he sobered up just enough to curse me for getting him into trouble with his wife.

I found his drinking and disgraceful behaviour deplorable, but it was the way he treated the horses that really bothered me. As the old saying goes, "There's something about the outside of a horse that tells you about the inside of a man."

Lightbulb was assigned Lancer, one of the kindest, most easygoing creatures you could ask for. A child could ride the animal, but Lightbulb kept the poor beast in a constant state of stress and anxiety.

He would ride through the streets holding the reins too tightly and digging his oversized spurs into the horse's flanks. Lancer would have to dance on the spot to accommodate Lightbulb's conflicting commands; he liked the image of himself on a prancing steed.

After what should have been a quiet ride, the horse would most often be returned to the stable dripping sweat and bleeding around the mouth. If no one else was at the stable, the horse would be put in his stall still wet and neglected.

The horses had to have the hair on their manes and legs clipped periodically and the job was the responsibility of the officer they were assigned to. Lancer would stand quietly when officers other than Lightbulb used the electric shears on him, but he insisted on using a painful device called a twitch clamped to the horse's muzzle and sometimes his ears.

Once when I saw this happening I offered to clip the horse for him, but he told me to fuck off and mind my own business. Being the junior man, I complied with his request.

If everybody at the station had been like him, working there would have been unbearable. But I was finding out that my initial impression of the men working on the unit had been wrong, and that, for the most part, they were good, hardworking guys and, if anything, slightly more sensitive than your average cop.

There was one man in particular whose personality stood out in stark contrast to the mean-spirited attitude of Lightbulb. His name was Frank Lepper. By the time I started with the unit he had already done his fair share of time on the street, over 35 years, and had opted to become Quartermaster, a role that would keep him in the stable mending tack; attending to sick or injured horses; and making sure that the unit was well supplied with all the special, sometimes hard-to-find, equipment that we needed.

He seemed very old to me when I first met him, but he couldn't have been too much more than fifty-five. Maybe it was the way he looked that had me pegging him as totally ancient. He was sitting in one of the old captain's chairs in the tack room with a yellow felt numnah spread over his lap, using a sewing awl to stitch away at a leather patch. His glasses were perched on the end of his nose and he looked for all the world like the illustrations of Geppetto in the Pinocchio books.

When he stood, rising to his full height, and took my hand, he defied this impression of frailness; his grip was not that of an old man; his hair was grey-white and his face had a few well-earned wrinkles, but he appeared slim and in good shape and with the bearing of a much younger man.

Frank was a crusty but likeable old hugger; a bit opinionated, but his opinions generally had a great deal of merit. He was like an old mother hen with the new men and wouldn't brook any nonsense from them; When one of them would get too big for their britches and start bragging about how well they could ride Frank would crank back at them, "You couldn't ride a street- car with the doors closed!"

He had a routine, every lunch hour he would finish up his dinner by eating an orange. You could always tell exactly how many horses were in the stable at the time by the number of pieces of orange peel that ended up in his thermos cup. When he was through eating he would go to each of the horses in their stalls and they would get their share of the peel from the flat of his hand.

I really liked him and looked upon him as a mentor. He was a wealth of knowledge about the mounted unit and his days on the R.C.M.P.

Sometimes, when Lightbulb was up to one of his nasty tricks with the horses, I would see Frank marching out of the stable shaking his head and rolling his eyes, but he would never take the man to task as he would have had it been anyone else. At first I couldn't figure out why Frank or, for that matter, the police force, would put up with a character like Light-bulb, but as time went on it became clear to me.

The man was a narcissistic sycophant of the first order. While it was understood that mounted policemen were to function, in most respects, like other members of the force, making arrests, traffic control etcetera, there was meant to be a strong emphasis on public relations. Everyone loved to see the horses on the streets. While the rest of our unit were do-ing their best to maintain a good rapport with locals, Lightbulb was ter-rorizing the neighbourhood by issuing literally hundreds of parking tick-ets every day. The stats looked good on the division's monthly reports and apparently were the reason that those in charge overlooked his mul-titude of sins.

I couldn't stand the man, and quite often, at the end of a shift when he walked through the lunchroom with his bony fingers clutched around a huge stack of yellow tickets, I would take him to task. I would say things like, "I hope you're proud of yourself!" or, 'How many people did you piss off today'?"

I think my remarks had caused him to dislike me, because one after-noon I was leaning back in a chair, writing in my memo book. When I saw him approaching with yet another huge pile of tickets I delivered another sarcastic salvo in his direction, then resumed writing.

When I looked up to see if my remarks had had any effect on him all I saw was a bundle of knuckles flying in my direction. Before I knew what was happening, I was on my back with Lightbulb hammering away at my head and shoulders.

I should mention that Lightbulb's life of debauchery had left him bereft of any muscle or conditioning that he once might have had, so it didn't take too much effort on my part to turn the tables on him and return a little bit of what he had been dishing out.

Our little disagreement was a signal for the rest of the cops present to leave the room and wait in the stable until we settled our differences. That's why, after we had rolled around the floor and exchanged punches for some considerable time, I was surprised to hear someone behind me cheering me on and shouting, "Give it to the bastard!"

Holding onto Lightbulb's skinny wrists, I glanced over my shoulder and saw that my vocal fan was not one of the other policemen. He was an irate citizen who had come to the station to complain about being repeatedly ticketed and harassed by Lightbulb.

His presence had a sobering effect on both my opponent and myself, so we unravelled long enough to direct him to the complaints department.

As the door closed behind him, I grabbed Lightbulb's shirtfront, pulled him toward me, and shouted, "You're under arrest for assault!"

He shoved me backwards and through clenched teeth growled, "Guess again, you little prick. *You're* under arrest!"

This debate might have gone on for some time, but it ended when the cold contents of three buckets of icy water came flying in our direction, followed by the rest of the crew. They separated us and explained how complicated it would be for us to arrest each other.

The water cooled me down and I realized how ridiculous we both had been acting, so I backed off and decided to let the matter drop.

Traditionally, what happens in the stable stays in the stable, so I went home for the weekend looking forward to letting bygones be bygones and resuming a normal routine. I hadn't considered the rodent-like tendencies of Lightbulb.

He contacted the Inspector at his home and shovelled his slanted version of what had happened into his willing ear. On Monday morning my horse remained tied up and instead I was riding the carpet in front of the Inspector's desk, defending myself.

Fortunately, I had recently received a commendation for a bit of clever police work and, bearing that in mind, he let the matter drop.

I hurried back to the stable, I was as mad as hell.

As I burst through the door I bumped into old Frank. "Where's Lightbulb?" I shouted. "I suppose he's up in the loft with the rest of the rats."

I tried to push by him, but he grabbed the door jam and blocked my way.

"Let it go, son, you can't win. I've seen lots of guys like Lightbulb over the years and eventually they get their comeuppance."

He was right, he always was, so I let the matter drop and decided to watch and wait.

A couple of years later, after I left the force, a policeman from Mounted Headquarters came to my door with the news that Lightbulb had been struck by a vehicle and killed when he had staggered out of his car on the busy 401 highway.

I asked when it had happened, and the cop said he wasn't sure, but that it must have a short time ago. He said he had been telephoned and asked to tell me about the accident by an old mounted cop who was now stationed at the Courts Bureau.

"You might know him," he said. "His name is Frank Lepper."

Frank Lepper

24: The precious new uniform

In celebration of Canada's Centennial year in 1967, everybody on the police force was issued with a new, colourful hat band to mark the occasion.

Inspector Johnson decided that a better tribute was required for the Mounted Unit, so he had a special dress uniform designed for us. It was a gaudy affair with bright- red accented lapels, and cuffs with clusters of white piping applied to blue serge jackets. Extra-wide, even redder, stripes were added to the britches, and all this was topped by a white pith helmet.

The Inspector explained that the department had gone to a lot of trouble and expense for the issue and that it would be a one-off gesture. Consequently we would have to take scrupulous care of our uniforms.

As luck would have it, I was the first to receive mine, and the Inspector made a big fuss about making me get dressed in it and having press photographers take pictures of me in all my splendour before sending me down to show it off at City Hall.

I remember him standing there, gleaming with pride, as I departed from the corner of Belmont and Davenport on my way to Bay Street, riding Roy. I felt like a clown in the flashy garb, but mine was not to reason why, so I pressed on, determined to keep the uniform, as directed, as clean and unsullied as possible.

Later in the afternoon, when it started to rain, Roy and I were able to shelter under the mezzanine in Nathan Phillips Square and protect my flashy new attire. I even declined the free coffee one of the venders offered me because Roy was fidgeting a bit and I didn't want to risk spilling it on myself.

The time to return to the stables came none too soon. I couldn't wait to get away from the hordes of tourist taking photos and asking why I looked like a Bengal Lancer.

I put Roy into a trot and headed north up Bay Street. He was eager for his evening oats and bran and didn't need much encouraging.

We had just zoomed through the intersection at Bloor Street when I noticed a crowd gathered in a vacant lot behind a tavern on Cumberland, just ahead. As we got closer it was evident that one of the frequent fights that were held in that location was in full swing.

Now, the police horse is a wonderful mediator in situations like that and on several previous occasions I had simply moved my horse in between the contestants and scowled down at them and they had stopped fighting and slipped away. There had been no need for me to get further involved.

As it turned out this simple, non-violent intervention was not going to work in this instance. The men were fighting ankle-deep in a large puddle and appeared to have been at it for a while. They both were smeared in mud and blood.

As the old saying goes, "A common danger will unite even the bitterest of enemies," and I was about to endure the validity of old Aristotle's prediction.

I moved Roy easily through the crowd and placed him between the two burly combatants, but instead of cowering away, both men decided to put aside their differences and join forces to attack me from two sides.

When they started punching Roy and yanking at his reins, I pulled out my little leather Billy, swung down and struck the man on my right on his head with such an impact that it burst its seams and sent a shower of the lead shot that weighted it into the puddle.

The fellow just shook his head, leapt up, grabbed the front of my jacket and started pulling me down. I might have managed to stop a downward plunge off the horse if the man on the other side hadn't grabbed my boot and shoved upward.

I flew off over Roy's head, landing flat out on my back in six inches of black ooze. Rolling over in the mud and slipping in my attempts to keep hold onto Roy's reins and get to my feet, I did manage at least to hold onto the reins.

Both combatants, now apparently the best of friends, took the opportunity to deliver a couple of parting kicks to my ribs, stomp and crush my helmet and then speed off into the distance.

I painfully mounted back up and was setting off for the stable just as a patrol car arrived. They said they would radio info about what had happened and set off looking for the men who had assaulted me.

Inspector Johnson was waiting, looking out of his office window when I arrived back. I was slumped over in the saddle, bruised and beaten, my torn, mud caked uniform unrecognizable and the remnant of my formerly white pith helmet suspended, dirty and battered, by its chinstraps from the pommel of my saddle. I can't vouch for it, but I think I saw tears in his eyes. I knew that they weren't out of concern for me, but for that darned uniform—his precious new pride and joy.

25: Singing in the rain

Recently I was looking for a picture of the old 57 Division Police Station when I happened on the following article posted by The Toronto Ghost and Haunting Society:

> *The following was recently submitted by one of our readers. What makes this report interesting* [is that] *it is the second report...we've received about this site. Both reports tell the same type and sort of phenomena about the stairs and the apparition of the woman.*
>
> *A police station was built on Davenport Rd. at the top of Bay Street at the turn of the century. The officers working this area patrolled the Annex and Yorkville area of Toronto. The station had stables attached and was for many years the lockup for female*

prisoners. In 1988 the building was partly demolished with the front remaining. It is now the headquarters of the Toronto Ambulance.

I was stationed at this location during the early 80's, and again when it finally closed as a police station. Many of the staff talked about the strange happenings during the nights. Footsteps up and down the staircase to the second floor. Several officers swore they had seen ghost-like figures of women. There were several women who had committed suicide in the cells in the early days. There was a loft area in the rear where hay was kept for the horses. I can remember hearing strange noises from this part of the building at night.

Of course, I was interested. I had spent three years working out of that old station. I don't believe in ghosts—well, maybe I do a little bit—and if I had to speculate on who the ghost in the article might be, I would instantly think of Irene.

In the 1960s Irene, no one knew her last name, was the best-known bag lady in the city. There was an aura of mystery about the woman. While she was obviously down and out, the way she carried herself and spoke suggested that she had once been used to living several steps higher on the social ladder. Her haughty, rapid, aristocratic banter reminded me of the way Katherine Hepburn spoke in her movies.

Irene wore, with a certain panache, second-hand but tastefully-selected clothes over her aged, anorexic frame, and walked as if she owned Yonge Street.

That's where Maloney introduced her to me, and I was to encounter her frequently, mostly in the late evening when she finished selling her roses to the departing theatre crowds.

One night, leaving work later than usual, I saw her about to set off for her digs—I never knew where—and in a moment of inspiration, I put my arm around her, and started singing:

Irene, good night, Irene.
Irene, good night.
Good night, Irene.
Good night, Irene.
I'll see you in my dreams.

She hummed along with the rest of the words of the old song, and then leaned in and gave me a peck on the cheek and said, "That was lovely, darling." She pronounced it 'dawling.'

Whenever we met after that, our parting would always be the same: me bellowing out "Good Night Irene", oftentimes with passing strangers joining in. Things didn't change much when I joined the Mounted Unit. When we'd meet at the end of her day, I'd dismount and she'd busy herself patting whatever horse I had with me while I sang.

She would never talk about her past, but there was one telling moment when she looked at my saddle and said, "I always rode side-saddle." That was a luxury mainly reserved for wealthy equestrians. But she was otherwise tight-lipped and wouldn't reveal anything about her past. It was as if she was running away from something or somebody.

One rainy night, late in the fall, I came upon her and Maloney in a heated conversation on the curb. She was totally drenched, her hair dishevelled, the cheap rouge and lipstick that she always wore smeared and running down her face.

I heard Maloney's voice first. "Now be reasonable, girl. You know I can't do dat. That jail up there isn't for a good woman like you. It's just for drunks and floozies."

Irene pleaded, "Please, Pat, I am a drunk."

"You ain't no drunk! Now stop this nonsense."

"I am," she shouted, digging into one of her shopping bags to produce a half-full bottle of cheap brandy. With determination she undid the top, tipped it back and gulped down the remainder. Pat had jumped forward to grab the bottle, but he was too late.

I quickly dismounted and rushed over to the pair. Irene was shivering so violently that I pulled off my raincoat and covered her.

She began whimpering an explanation for her behaviour. "I can't go home. My next-door neighbour at the rooming house found me and told me that a man got out of a big luxury car and came to the door looking for me. He said the man said he was my son and had been looking for me for years. I can't go there. I can't let him see what has become of me. I deserted him when he was a baby. I had to. For God's sake, Pat, just take me to jail. I hope I never get out. Please, please!"

Maloney and I conferred for a moment or two and agreed that he would transport her to 57 Division while I talked to the duty sergeant, making sure she was kept safe and secure from the general population of the jail.

Pat had her seated in the cab of the wagon with him and I had mounted up when Irene rolled down the passenger window and said, "Aren't you forgetting something?"

"Oh yeah!" I broke into song. "*Irene, good night, Irene. Irene, good night...*"

The rain kept pouring down and I kept singing while the paddy wagon disappeared in the distance.

Maloney had arrived, left Irene and gone out in his paddy wagon by the time I rode in. The duty officer had willingly made exceptions for Irene. Everybody on the job knew her. He hadn't even searched her, and he let her take her bags with her up to the cell on second floor.

When I got back to the stables the next day, the old stable man, Frank Lepper, informed me that Irene had hung herself during the night.

Maybe now, if they are still wondering who the ghost might be, when they hear footsteps in the night in the old station, they should try singing 'Irene, Good Night' and listen for someone humming along.

26: A quiet man on Cowan Avenue

I first met Mrs. Macintyre when I was nine years old. Her first name was Margret but she insisted that I call her Maggie.

She lived with her husband, Lee, a former regimental sergeant in the Toronto Scottish, in a neat three-story brick house on Cowan Avenue in the Parkdale area of Toronto. We lived in a rented house further along the street and I was the Macintyres' paper delivery boy and go-to kid for odd jobs around their place.

I always looked forward to the days when she would call to me from her veranda to tell me that Lee would be away for a couple of days and that the lawn needed mowing and there were oak leaves in the backyard that needed attention. "Lee's workshop could use a little tiding up, but best leave that to him...you know how fussy he is around his tools."

I knew too well how particular he was about his shop. One day he caught me exploring, picking up and admiring the tools on his bench, and lost his temper and bellowed at me in the manner he been accustomed to use during his time in WWII.

I was shocked because, until that incident, I had known him as the gentle, quiet giant of a man whom I had often seen striding out of his door decked out in his Todden Grey kilt, his breast bristling with medals and ribbons.

"Pay no attention," Maggie had said. "Lots of men have come back from the war different from when the left. So many things they are trying to forget and so many things they can never tell you. I'm sure he appreciates the help you give me when he is away."

"Why is he away so often?" I innocently asked.

"Well, sonny, I'm sure you saw some of those signs that were around during the war. 'Loose lips sink ships.' The war's been over for quite a while, but Lee is still in the reserve and he is frequently called in to meet with certain people. He won't tell me what it's all about and I don't ask. The extra money he makes help pay for the work little rascals like you get paid."

Two years later we moved away from the neighbourhood, but over the ensuing years I would occasionally drop in to see how the couple were getting on. But then life got in the way and I lost touch with them

One day, years later, I was in the guard room of the police station I was serving at when I happened on the obituaries in the *Toronto Star* and saw that Regimental Sergeant Lee Macintyre, after a long illness, had passed away at Sunnybrook Veterans Hospital and that ceremonies would be held at the Royal Canadian Legion on the following Tuesday.

I took a quick look at the date on the paper. It was a week old,.I had missed the funeral, but I felt I should do something. Maybe I could bring Maggie a paper or offer to mow the lawn.

I didn't take the time to change out of my uniform. I stopped for a moment at a local store to buy a newspaper and some flowers and headed straight to Cowan Avenue.

She was awhile making her way to the door, and shocked to be confronted with a policeman with flowers in one hand and newspaper in the other.

When I tilted my hat back, she immediately recognized me and invited me into the house. "Where have you been? It's been ages."

Later, over the tea and cookies she had produced out of nowhere, she said, "As you might have noticed, I have a man to look after the maintenance of the yard now, but I don't know what to do with all that clutter in Lee's shop. Would you come out there with me? Maybe there's something you would like to remember the cranky old guy who chased you out of there."

We both laughed, then I agreed, and we made our way out to the shop.

It was the way I remembered it, still neatly arranged, though a bit dusty and clung here and there with cobwebs.

"Pick anything you want, dear. The rest is going to Waddington's Auction House tomorrow."

I was caressing an antique block plane when a large metal chest with padlock caught my eye. "What's in the chest, Maggie?"

"I don't know. The auction company man didn't open it."

"I don't like the sound of that. You know how auctioneers are. There could be something really valuable in there. You never know."

Looking around I spied a vintage pair of bolt cutters. "Should I open it for you?"

"No harm in that. Go ahead; cut away."

Maggie noticed someone arriving in her yard and excused herself to go out and greet him. She seemed like she would be involved with her visitor for a while, so I decided to open the chest and take a look.

As expected, it was neatly packed. Two piles of papers covered something hidden below.

A newspaper was spread prominently over one pile boasting a headline that was familiar.

> Arthur Lucas and Ronald Turpan hung back-to-back. December 11 1962 at Toronto's Don Jail.

Beside the newspapers was a pile of Canadian Army court martial directives for execution by firing squad. When I lifted the papers aside, I found something that made my blood run cold.

Coiled together were several hemp ropes, two of which were tied into traditional hangman's knots. Tucked in amongst them were several black hoods.

Realizing what I had discovered, I immediately slammed the top down and headed out to where Maggie was waiting. "Hey, Maggie, that trunk is empty. If you don't mind, I would like to have it to store my tools in at home."

She was agreeable, so while she went into the house to prepare yet another pot of tea, I hefted the trunk out to my car and put it in the trunk.

When I got it home and had more time, I found that the contents of the trunk told a story of their own.

The papers containing orders for firing squads suggested that Lee Macintyre had acquired his skill for conducting fellow soldiers to their maker during the war, and that it was later that he honed his expertise with the rope.

Apparently, his talent in this regard was much in demand. There was a 1946 letter requesting him to assist at the multiple hangings of convicted war criminals at Nuremburg in October of that year.

With credentials like that, a simple two-man hanging at the Don Jail should have been a walk in the park for him, but I had heard otherwise. An old cop I once worked with told me he was present at the execution and spun me a horrible tale.

The two back-to-back men, as was the prescribed custom, were given the last rites, hooded, fitted with their nooses then dropped through a trap door down to the next floor, where the executioner waited. If necessary, he would jump up, pounce on them, then embrace and hang on to the quivering bodies so his extra weight would hasten their death.

As my informant put it, it was not all that simple and there was a lot of blood and gore to deal with when it was over.

He said he never knew the name of the hangman. It was always a well-kept secret.

But now I knew who he was, and it was hard to accept that he was the quiet, unassuming old soldier I had once known. What really struck home with me was a document showing that he presided over the execution of the cop killers Steve Suchan and Lennie Jackson in 1952....around the time he chased me out of his workshop.

I took the metal trunk out to my backyard, planning to put the contents in my burn barrel ,but on second thought, since it was a strong metal container and I didn't want to touch the contents, I opted to simply raise the lid, pour some kerosene inside and set it ablaze. No one else, especially Maggie, needed to ever know what was fuelling the fire.

As I stood alone watching the flames rise higher, I thought of it as a fitting way to quietly celebrate the end of Capital Punishment in Canada.

If you search online for the name of the last hangman in Canada, no name turns up... no one seems to know.

But I do...at least I think I do.

27: An owl for the shooting

An owl has taken up residence close to our Nova Scotia place to take advantage of the "all you can eat" menu of Guinea hen chicks that we own but have no control over. There were about sixteen hatched out this summer, but every day when we could get close enough to count them one or more would be missing.

We are now down to one half-grown chick, protected by four adults. We always try to get them into the hen house, but it is nearly impossible.

I have tried to reason with the owl whenever I catch sight of him, brandishing my rifle and yelling threats, but he doesn't give a hoot. He knows he is probably on the endangered species list. He just winks at me in a most condescending manner, like he owns the place.

I don't like owls, and my animosity was engendered toward them more than half a century ago when one of the supposedly-wise old buggers could have caused me to lose my job on the police force.

When winter descended on the city in 1964, those of us on the Mounted Unit dug out our winter garb—special great coats with enough extra length to drape over the horse's rump and divert a bit of animal heat up in the direction of the rider's back. Also there were no more thin, tight leather boots, just bulky felt things we called Russian socks slipped into short, rubber galoshes and held in place by our spur straps. Not pretty, but really warm.

During the previous winter, my first on the Mounted Unit, the one spot on my body that was not adequately protected was my head. All we wore was a regular thin forage cap with ear flaps.

That's why we were all excited and grateful when Inspector Johnson presented us with very expensive, heavily-lined Persian lamb hats, although I noticed a bit of hesitation when he handed me mine. Surely he wasn't still harbouring a grudge over the incident with my dress uniform?

Anyway, the winter progressed uneventfully until the following spring, when disaster struck. I was riding through Mount Pleasant Cemetery when something struck me on the head with great force. At first, I thought someone had hit me with a stone, but when I looked up, I saw a Great Horned owl flying toward the horizon with my fur hat clutched in his talons.

A desirable winter hat

Blood from gashes on my head was dripping into my eyes, but I spurred my horse on, trying to catch him or find where he might land. It was to no avail and, after three hours of riding around scanning the graveyard's treetops, I found myself riding home bareheaded.

Of course, as usual around the end of shift time, Inspector Johnson was watching from his window, eyeing our arrival. I was toast. Any explanation I could offer would sound like "the dog ate my homework".

He didn't rush down to confront me. Instead, he took the time to dig out the old invoices from the purchase of the new hats, scratched out a bill for $80.00 and brought it down to me. That was a lot of money in those days, maybe a week's pay but I decided to quietly suck it up and bring him a cheque. I didn't dare tell him about the owl.

A few weeks earlier another constable, let's call him Andy Britton, had come to the Inspector with a story about he had lost his hat to an owl. Apparently, it was the last straw in a series of shenanigans Constable Britton was involved in, so he was immediately fired. As a result of that, I thought it best to keep my owl story under close wraps until, much later, in a weak moment while inebriated at the squad's Christmas party, I finally told my owl story to the Inspector.

As expected, he didn't believe a word of it, but since I had accidentally done some exceptional police work in the previous week, he decided to assume I was making a joke, referencing PC Britton's cock and bull story about an owl, and just laughed it off.

Whenever I subsequently got sent to patrol in that graveyard wearing my new expensive second hat, I rode round with one hand on it and the other ready to drop the reins and grab my revolver. That pesky owl would not get away with it twice.

I assumed the matter had been long forgotten when, three months later Inspector Johnson called me into his office.

"The caretaker from Mount Pleasant Cemetery came in this morning and presented me with these," he said, pointing to two crumpled-up, threadbare Persian lamb hats. "He said that they had had an arborist in to trim some dead branches from one of their big old trees and he had found these near the top in what appeared to be a nest, and thought I might be interested. The tag is difficult to read but it appears to say PC 754 and I believe that's you. I can't read the other tag, but I guess we both know whose hat that would be. I believe an apology is in order. I can't repay the money you spent on the new hat, so I'm giving you the equivalent in days off. As for Britton, he's long gone, and his owl adventure was the least of his problems."

I never got the opportunity to get my gun out and get even with that owl in the graveyard, and now five decades later, here I am, still forced to keep my pistol holstered while our new resident raptor, playing his endangered species card, terrorizes our poultry with impunity.

28: A messy business

Okay, I'll admit it: when I was a policeman on the Toronto Mounted Unit in the 1960s, I really enjoyed the attention I got when I rode through the busy streets of the city. It was as though my horse and I were a glimpse of the past, something almost ethereal amidst the chaos. I was always pumped up with pride as we pranced along, turning heads and putting smiles on children's faces.

With Old Major

But as wonderful as it was, I had to make the most of those moments because I knew that, at some point my horse would stop, lift his tail and deposit a steaming offering on the pavement, and the vision would fade. Children would gag and grownups would hustle by trying not to notice.

It always seemed to happen at the most inopportune moments and often in regrettable locations, and when it did, all I could do was appear quietly detached and try to maintain my dignity.

In those days, city people still kept gardens and needed fertilizer, so these random offerings left curbside were not much of a problem. However, there were unusual situations in this regard that sorely tested the otherwise good relationship the Mounted Unit enjoyed with the public.

One day, while I was in the saddle writing a parking ticket on a quiet residential street, my mount took the opportunity to register his contempt for flashy vehicles by voiding into the driver's seat of a convertible sports car.

My first instinct was to flee the scene and hope that the blame would fall on some other horse, but since the only horses left in the city belonged to the Police Force, I realized that that idea wouldn't fly. For a moment I thought that if I left immediately it would be hard to trace the infraction to any specific police mount, but as I looked down on the prodigious volume of the glistening heap, I knew that only one horse in the stables was capable of producing a plop of that magnitude and I was sitting on him.

Old Major was a favourite of the Inspector, and because he was coddled so much the horse was grossly overweight. He regularly consumed as much hay and oats as two or three of the other horses combined.

No, they wouldn't have to call in the detectives to determine who the guilty party was in this case.

I wrote an apologetic note on the back of a cancelled parking ticket and slipped it under the car's windshield wiper, then headed back to the stable to fess up. The duty sergeant wasn't too happy when I gave him my report, and by the way he reprimanded me you would have thought it was I and not Major who had dumped in the MG.

I left the old horse in his stall for the rest of that afternoon and, armed with every cleaning device the station had to offer, I returned to the scene of the crime and cleaned up the mess. The car's owner was very understanding and, coincidentally, after that day he never seemed to get any more parking tickets.

While the uninhibited police horses were free to urinate, defecate and break wind with impunity anywhere they wanted, it was a different matter for those who rode them. In the old days, when lots of city dwellers were familiar with horses, it was a simple matter of recruiting a willing citizen to hold your horse while you went into a washroom to relieve yourself, but by the sixties these handy volunteers were few and far between.

It was the practice of most of the policemen to visit the toilet at the stables just before they went out on patrol, but being caught short was still always a possibility, particularly for some of the older members of the unit. If we were patrolling a park and there weren't too many people around, we could always dismount behind a bush for a quick whiz, but if we had more serious business to attend to, things could be difficult. The horses weren't equipped with sirens for emergency runs back to the station.

My fellow constable Ron Bond was patrolling a park one summer day when a series of fierce stomach cramps demanded immediate attention. There was an outhouse close to a kids' playground. The area was crowded but he didn't see anyone who looked like they could hold his horse, so, ever resourceful, my buddy came up with a plan whereby he could use the facility and hold his horse at the same time.

This would be termed multi-tasking today.

Trying not to draw too much attention to himself, he dismounted and quietly led his horse over to the latrine, then, checking that nobody was looking, turned around and sheepishly backed through the door. He kept the reins in his hands and, being careful not to scare the horse, partially closed the door and then set about his business.

I don't know how long he was in there, but at some point someone or something spooked his horse. The wild-eyed animal reared and lurched backwards, and my friend, forced to obey the cardinal rule of never letting go of your horse, held on for dear life.

He was catapulted through the outhouse door with his britches and boxer shorts draped around his ankles, and then dragged a considerable distance over the turf before he got his horse stopped.

While startled mothers shrieked and shielded their children's eyes, the red-faced cop slipped behind his horse, pulled up his drawers and regained his composure. Then he mounted up and, saluting the assembled crowd, rode off as if nothing had happened.

The Mounted Unit is still going strong in Toronto and I am sure they have benefited greatly by the advances in technology the last forty or so years have provided, but horses still do what horses have always done and riders still have basic needs to look after, so in that respect I'll bet nothing much has changed.

29: Another game of Zeaton Ball

One morning in 1967 I found myself in the company of eleven other mounted policemen making our way through the backstreets of downtown Toronto on our way to the American Consulate on University Avenue. We were mounted on the quietest, most experienced horses that the force had to offer. I had been assigned Buccaneer, the best of them all.

Before we set out that morning we were informed that we were going on a crowd control mission at an antiwar demonstration in front of the Consulate. "We have to be prepared for anything." the Sergeant said, reminding us of some the problems our American counterparts were having at similar demonstrations in New York and other major centres.

We had seen the training films and read the reports of police horses being attacked by radical demonstrators. Some of them had used straight razors taped to the ends of hockey sticks to slash the horses and their riders, and there were instances where thousands of ball bearings were hurled onto the pavement, causing the horses to lose their footing and crash to the ground. The injuries to animals and their riders were horrendous.

The thought of something similar happening here haunted me as we rode along, but I comforted myself with the thought that, "This is Canada. People don't behave that way here." At least I hoped they didn't.

When we arrived at a little side street close to the Embassy, we dismounted and checked our equipment. We had a minimal amount of tack on the horses, no fancy breastplates or lanyards, nothing for troublemakers to get hold of should things get out of hand.

We had just tightened the horse's girths and shortened their curb chains when the order came to mount up. Something was developing. Hordes of chanting, placard-carrying protesters were pouring down University Avenue, filling the sidewalk and spilling over onto the street in front of the Consulate.

We rode up closer to the scene and sat two abreast, watching. The fifty or so policemen on foot seemed to have things under control and were not meeting with much resistance as they gently ushered people out of the roadway. Buccaneer and I were closest to curb and he stood quietly as people brushed by us on their way to join the protest.

Over the chanting and the shouts, I heard someone close by call my name. I looked down and, pressed in close to me, almost touching my riding boot, was an old classmate of mine, Richard Ilomacky.

"What's happening?" I shouted. "What are you doing here?" Silly question, since he was carrying a sign with some pretty strong antiwar sentiments.

It was too noisy for conversation, so I gave him the old 'catch you later' sign and he walked on, disappearing into the crowd. I knew Richard fairly well; we both had attended a tough inner-city high school, Central Tech, and had taken P.T. classes together.

Our gym teacher was a tough ex-policeman who had been selected by the Board of Education more for his brawn than his brains. He thought that most conventional sports were too tame so he invented his own game and named it after himself.

The rules for Zeaton Ball were very simple. The class, after dividing itself into two teams, faced each other from opposite ends of the gym. Mr. Zeaton would then roll a basketball into centre court and, at the sound of his whistle, the teams would charge at each other. The object of the game was to get the ball down to your opponent's end of the gym and score a basket, by any means possible. No dribbling, penalty shots or off-sides were required, and the more tripping, kicking, and punching that went on, the better he liked it. Quite often he would simply drift off and leave the class to its own devices.

His one and only rule was that when the game was over, it was over, and heaven help anyone who continued to fight or even appeared to be holding a grudge afterwards.

Ilomacky and I had locked horns in these contests many times before the Principal caught wind of what was going on and stopped them.

I was standing in my stirrups, trying to see where my old friend had gone, when the whole gathering seemed to turn as one from facing the Consulate to focusing their attention on several buses with American license plates that were pulling up on the opposite side of the street.

The American Legion was making an unexpected visit. Hundreds of Legionnaires poured out of the buses and took up positions opposite the antiwar group. There was a great deal of shouting and placard rattling back and forth, but things, for a time, looked like they might remain calm, cool and Canadian.

Then somebody threw something,, and shortly the air was full of missiles, hundreds of rocks, fruit and pop cans landing and being returned. Then the two factions began to converge, and we knew that all hell was about to break out.

The newspapers the next day claimed that somebody had yelled, 'Charge!' I didn't hear it, but charge we did, attempting to put our horses between the two groups.

As we forced our way up the centre line of University Avenue, I encountered Ilomacky again. He had just smashed his placard over the head of a Legionnaire and, as I approached him, he thrust the sharp broken end of the stick at me, hitting me in the chest.

I reached out to grab him, almost losing my seat in the saddle, but he slipped from my grasp and got away. I wanted to chase him, but I knew that the Sergeant had other plans for me.

By this time, we had formed a solid line of nose-to-tail horses between the worst combatants of the two groups. The Sergeant shouted the command for a Side Passage and, moving perfectly sideways, crossing their legs as they went, the horses swept the angry crowds from the roadway and back to their own sides of the street. Pockets of hand-to-hand fighting were still breaking out on both sides of the street, but about one hundred foot-patrol policemen were now on the scene and the paddy wagons had begun to arrive.

Maloney's wagon was parked close to me and I was watching him as he loaded some of the more violent protesters who had been arrested. That's when I saw a struggling Ilomacky being hustled by three constables over to the back of the wagon. They passed him off to Maloney, who held him easily with one of his big hands.

He was about to fling him into the vehicle when I caught his eye. Not sure of why I was doing it, I shook my head and indicated that I wanted him to let him go.

With a 'who cares' look on his face, Maloney spun my friend around and planted a size fourteen boot in his arse that sent him reeling into the crowd.

Before he totally disappeared, Ilomacky glanced back at me with a quizzical look on his face. It was as if he was saying, "Who's side are you on?"

To tell the truth, I wasn't sure myself. If he could have heard me, I would have said, "Just think of it as another game of Zeaton Ball."

30: The King and I

In the 1960s we didn't have street people in Toronto. We had good, old-fashioned bums, hobos and vagrants. The mental institutions like the one at 999 Queen Street West had yet to fling open their doors and herd droves of temporarily-medicated inmates into the streets; There were only a few real loonies wandering around and they, for the most part, were harmless and added a little colour and interest to the downtown area.

There was one fellow who we called Lazarus. He looked like Rasputin, with the added touch of hugely-distended nostrils, which he kept stuffed with great wads of newspaper. He used to cruise the streets, summer and winter, clad in a dirty old overcoat and a pair of gym shorts, stopping at every fire hydrant, kneeling and sneezing at it three times.

When I ask him once why he performed his ritual, he said simply, "Purification."

I didn't delve into the matter any further. One didn't hang around Lazarus too long; he always was enveloped in a cloud of pong sufficient to gag a maggot.

Most of the vagrants I met were simply down and out alcoholics who bummed money for booze during the day and slept their binges off during their nights at the Sally Ann or one of the other shelters. The only time that the police paid much attention to them was when the city was going to host a special event or something like a royal visit. Then we would be told that the city fathers would like the unsavoury characters out of site for a while.

It wouldn't take long until the drunk tanks were full to bursting with inebriants. Most of those arrested were feeling no pain and would hardly know where they were until the booze wore off.

There was very little animosity between the police and the bums; the bums knew the cops were just doing their job and the cops, many of whom were closet alcoholics themselves, realized that "there, but for the grace of God, go I."

When the vagrants were arrested, they most often had large bottles of cheap booze in their possession and this would have to be confiscated. It was common practice for lots of caring cops to let the bums swallow most of the remaining booze before putting them in the cells. "Just leave me about half an inch in the bottom for evidence," they would say, and the bum was more than happy to oblige.

As amicable as the bum/cop relationship could be, you still had to be careful when dealing with guys you weren't familiar with. Sometimes some pretty tough, dangerous guys used Skid Row as a convenient hiding place.

One afternoon I was on mounted patrol in centrally-located Allen Gardens, a favourite hangout for bums and transients. Most of the time, it was just a question of riding through and making your presence known; the regular batch of boozers were usually well behaved and adept at keeping their bottles put of sight.

I was riding King, a big half-Belgian gelding. He was a handsome horse; he had a shiny chestnut coloured body with light mane and tail. He was a bit nervous and flighty, but I liked riding him.

As we entered the park, it was immediately apparent that something unusual was going on. A crowd had gathered in the centre court, near the water fountain, and as we rode closer I could see over their heads to where a large, bearded man was assaulting one of the old regulars and stealing his wine bottle.

King pushed his way through the crowd, and when the big, scraggy man saw us approaching, he threw the wine bottle in our direction. It, missed smashing against the concrete base of the water fountain.

He turned to run away, but the crowd slowed him down, and seconds later King was breathing on the back of his neck.

I thought he was about to give up, but instead he spun around, grabbed King's bridle and started punching the horse repeatedly on his muzzle. I tried to back the horse away, but the man hung on to the bridle and continued hitting him.

King, in terror, reared, lifting the man, who was still holding onto bridle, high off the ground. When King's front feet returned to the ground one of his heavy hooves was planted firmly in the middle of his assailant's chest, pinning him to the ground.

I dismounted and lifted the horse's hoof off the man, but he wasn't moving and, worst of all, he wasn't breathing.

"Oh my God!" I thought. "I can't just let him die."

Actually, I could have, but there were too many witnesses around and it would require a lot of explaining. So, reluctantly, I let my St. John's Ambulance training kick in;

I gave King's reins to the closest pair of hands that I could see; knelt beside the man and, after positioning his head, prepared to give him mouth to mouth. It took all my courage and resolve to place my mouth over that grizzly toothless hole, but somehow, holding back the gags, I managed to do it.

I blew into him once, but my breath just seemed to come back at me. Obviously there was some kind of blockage. I took a deep breath and went down on him again, determined to give it everything I had.

This time I felt something move but, before I realized what was happening, a torrent of sour, lumpy vomit projected into my mouth.

I staggered to my feet spitting and gagging and throwing up myself.

That's when Sergeant Weir made his appearance. He had been watching the whole incident and had already radioed for an ambulance and some backup.

He held King while I went to the nearby fountain and repeatedly rinsed my mouth. There wasn't enough water in the world.

After the Sergeant confided in me that he would have let the man die, he sent me home early so that I could stop at the drug store and stock up on mouthwash and disinfectant.

It was a long time before I ever really felt clean again. Even as I write this story, forty-five years later, I feel compelled to go and gargle and brush my teeth.

31: Who knew? *or* How my horse and I unwittingly helped get our Canadian hate laws improved

On the morning of June 19, 1966, in the company of a dozen or so other members of our mounted unit, I rode my horse into Allen Gardens in Toronto. We were there to put ourselves between the two groups: a neo-Nazi named John Beattie, who had come to speak, accompanied by his gang of brown shirts; and the hordes of protesters who came to confront him.

All hell broke loose the moment he started to speak. Young men from Israeli-backed organizations attempted to breach the lines of cops to get at the Nazis. Scores of older Jewish men and women began keening, screaming and exposing their concentration camp tattoos. There was chaos everywhere and individual fights started at different locations away from the main confrontation.

We, the Mounted Unit, were ordered to break ranks and spur our mounts off to deal with these isolated situations. As usual, it didn't take long to quell the trouble once the horses appeared. There were a few arrests and, until recently, I had stored that troubled day in my "Been there done that" file.

I didn't realize it at the time, but I have recently discovered, to my pleasure, that, on that day in the park, my horse and I were a small part of an elaborate plot hatched by The Canadian Jewish Congress (CJC) to draw attention to the need for stricter hate laws. That's right: groups that were opposed to the Nazis had actually encouraged the event. They wanted to bring the issue of hate crimes to the forefront because it was being debated in Parliament at that time.

It turns out that an ex-cop named John Garrity had been hired as a spy by the CJC to infiltrate the Nazi Party and help John Beattie gain prominence, so that later he could be used as a dupe in their cause. He was a

119

twenty-four-year-old unemployed clerk, a loser who posed no real threat to anyone. The meeting in the park was just an elaborate ruse to high-light the need for improvement of the country's hate legislation.

Of course, no one, least of all myself, realized that this wasn't a real re-surgence of Nazism. I give credit to those who devised the ploy, because it worked. Canadians all over the country reaffirmed their stand against the Nazis and all they stood for, and the CJC succeeded in getting the le-gislation they hoped for:

Section 319 (1) of the Criminal Code states that hate speech "incites hatred against any identifiable group where such incitement is likely to lead to a breach of the peace" and where the comments are made in a public place.

32: Brucie smiles at everyone

Brucie in board

56 Division was situated on Pape Avenue in the east end of Toronto. It was a typical old-style police station, a solid brick structure with a garage to one side and a large stable at its rear. It was one of the many similar facilities throughout the city scheduled to be decommissioned and torn down.

The sturdy old building had stood the test of time and, had it been able to speak, what a tale it would have told.

At its inception it had been manned by big, bobby-helmeted constables who walked the beats in the neighbourhood and actually knew and were known by the people they were supposed to serve and protect. Most of the minor crimes in those days never reached the courtrooms. The men on the beat dealt out a form of summary justice, which amounted to a good boot in the arse for juvenile delinquents and stern, sometimes physical, reprimands for wife beaters. There were few reoffenders.

All of that was now in the past. As the new, centralized stations rose on their foundations, these faithful old symbols of the law were being left, with minimal maintenance, to decay and pass away. Soon the neighbourhood could look forward to occasional visits from scout cars driven by policemen who needed a city map to find their way around the area.

I wasn't excited or particularly happy about my temporary assignment to the old station, but I knew that the surrounding area was ideal for schooling the young horses I was working with. It had busy streets with streetcars, buses and any number of the other strange vehicles that the remounts would have to become accustomed to. It also had the huge parks near the Don River, where the horses could canter off some of their youthful exuberance.

As I entered the stable on my first morning, my two horses and the other six that shared the stable were already nickering for their breakfast. I stowed my kit bag in the tack room and doled out a generous helping of oats and bran to each horse. Feeding the horses was always the responsibility of the first man in.

I had just returned to where I had left my gear and was writing in my memo book when I heard the door to the stable open and close. I shifted my position and craned my neck to see who was coming in.

I didn't know anyone at the station and was about to get up and introduce myself when, through the doorway, I saw someone walk towards the row of tall green lockers that lined the wall. He acted as if he owned the place and went directly to one locker and opened the door. He hadn't noticed me and the only part of him that I could see was his back. He didn't look big enough to be a policeman; he was just a teenage boy.

"Hi, who are you?" I asked.

He didn't seem startled and, turning towards me with a sweet smile on his face, said, "Me Brucie where Cy?"

The boy was obviously special and had the characteristics associated with Downs Syndrome.

I said that I didn't know where Cy was, and watched as he kicked his way out of pair of old running shoes, dropped his drawers and squirmed out of the tattered T shirt he was wearing. He seemed oblivious to my presence as he began pulling clothing out of the locker and dressing himself in some pretty respectable duds.

When he finished dressing, he took a toothbrush and some paste from the top shelf of the locker and went over to the horse trough and brushed his teeth. Returning to the locker, he pulled a comb through his hair and then closed the door.

My curiosity was just beginning to peak when the stable door swung open once again and an older policeman hurried over to the boy and handed him a brown paper bag.

"I'm sorry I'm late," he said. "Here's your lunch. You better hurry along."

As Brucie left the stable, the cop, who seemed to be playing mother, noticed me sitting in the other room and came over to introduce himself. "Hi. I'm Cy."

I had already figured that much out myself, but I was really anxious to find out more about the scene I had just witnessed.

Being a new man at the station, I didn't want to ask too many questions, but I was surprised Cy never offered any explanation concerning Brucie. In fact, he avoided the subject altogether and simply told me about the other men I would be working with and described the various patrol routes we used.

More of the crew began to arrive, but they never mentioned Brucie either, and I was still reticent to ask about him. I had to wait until the end of the day to find out what was going on.

It was quitting time and we were on our way to our cars when one of the guys confided in me. He told me that Brucie was Cy's project; he had sort of adopted the boy.

The relationship had started one day when Cy was on horseback, patrolling one the many back lanes in the area. He heard laughter coming from behind a backyard board fence, and when he stood in his stirrups and peered over the barrier, he startled a group of teenage girls who were crowded around, fondling a very naked and crying Brucie.

By the time Cy had dismounted and made his way into the yard, the girls had all disappeared and the very upset boy was leaning on the fence, sobbing. Cy gathered up the boy's clothes and helped him to get dressed, then, with the boy on one side and his horse on the other, he walked to where the boy said he lived.

He wasn't very impressed with the reception he got from Brucie's parents. They acted like they didn't care about what had happened and, as he looked at the eleven brothers and sisters who were crowding in the doorway, he thought he recognized two of the girls he had seen molesting the boy.

The proper thing to do would be to call Child Welfare, but Cy was old school and didn't relish the thought of the boy ending up in an institution. He thought that it would be better if he kept an eye on the situation himself and made sure the kid wasn't mistreated in the future.

Brucie was always wearing shabby hand-me-downs, and since Cy knew that the boy was attending a special school and would be a likely target for teasing, he decided to buy him some more suitable clothes.

Brucie looked pretty spiffy the first few mornings as he passed the station on his way to school, but it wasn't long before he was back in his old rags and his brothers and sisters were all wearing pieces of his new wardrobe.

That's when Cy decided to give the boy his own locker at the stables and bought him another set of clothing. Each morning before school Brucie would come and change.

The new arrangement was working well, and Cy even addressed the matter of the boy's personal hygiene, buying him a toothbrush and toothpaste and insisting that the boy take regular baths in the horse trough.

By the time I arrived at the stables, the arrangement, with the collaboration of the other cops assigned there, had been going on for several months. The boy seemed very happy and always had a smile for everybody as he went through his daily routine.

I had been working at the station for about three weeks when, one day, I found out that things had changed. Brucie came to the station in the afternoon and, with tears in his eyes, announced that he and his family were moving. Family Services had decided to move them out of the hovel they had been living in and place them in a house in the extreme west end of the city. It was more than an hour's ride away on a streetcar and an almost impossible distance to walk.

It was a sad day when Cy helped Brucie empty his locker and pack his few belongings into a cardboard box. He turned the boy over to his parents and hoped that, now that Social Services were involved, things might be alright.

Several weeks of a long hot summer had passed since we said goodbye to Brucie, and on one of the hottest days of all I came in off patrol and saw Brucie staggering into the stable yard. He looked exhausted; he must have been walking for hours.

As he got closer I could see that he was holding something in his arms.

"Where's Cy? I want show Cy my pup," he said.

Draped over his arm was a large Collie puppy, glassy eyed and very dead.

He kept stroking the puppy and asking for Cy as I helped him into the stable and found him a chair.

Cy was in the main station, turning in his gun and memo book, and when I told him about Brucie and the pup he said, "You go home, I'll handle this."

It was my last day at the station and I never saw or talked to Cy again, but I have never forgotten my last glimpse through the stable door. Framed in the tack room doorway, a large policeman knelt in front of a boy seated in a chair, holding a dead puppy in his arms. The man's big hand is covering the boy's as they caress the pup and the old cop searches for something to say.

Several years later, after I left the police force, I was shopping at a farmer's market in Stoufville, a town north of Toronto, when a mini bus pulled up and several people from a group home piled out and headed for the food stalls. The last person out of the bus must have been in charge of the home mascot, because he held a beautiful Border Collie dog on a leash. As he passed me our eyes met and his face broke into a wide smile.

I know he didn't really recognize me. Brucie smiles at everyone.

33: Joe was a nudger

Horses are like people. They all have distinctive personalities and some have peculiar habits. For example, police mount Stewart, a red bay gelding with a white blaze and a roman nose, was a Star Gazer, which meant that he liked to travel around with his head thrown back looking skyward. King, a golden chestnut with white main and tail, was a Fiddle Foot; he liked to dance on the spot whenever you stopped him.

Old Major, as well as being a mooch, was obsessed with pawing the pavement. You would have to hold him with both hands whenever somebody passed by with a bag of groceries in their arm, especially if he smelt apples or carrots. He would start nickering in a pleading tone and often people who knew him would give him a treat.

Whenever you stopped him at an intersection he would become impatient while waiting for the light to change and start pawing the pavement. If there were a bunch of kids on the sidewalk waiting for the light, I would shout as I reined him in, "How old are you Major?" and he would start pawing. He was usually about twenty by the time the light changed, and we moved on.

Some the habits the horses acquired were amusing, but others were downright annoying. Take for example Joe. He was a nudger, every time you tried to groom him or put his bridle on he would persistently bump you with his nose. There was nothing he liked better than to pin you up against a stall wall and, lovingly, nudge the hell out you. It didn't matter who you were or what you did to avoid it, he would have his nose up against you, nuzzling away. Even if you gave him a whack he would just look startled and hurt for a second or two and then be right back at it.

He wasn't much to look at, just a plain old bay with a white star on his forehead, but once you got him tacked up and were on his back he was a pleasure to ride because he was fearless. Nothing bothered him, not buses or streetcars or trains or motorcycles; he was immune to the things that terrified many of the other horses.

One rainy evening I was out on Joe patrolling south on Yonge Street, Toronto's main drag. I was wearing my big black rain-coat, which covered me and draped over Joe's rump, keeping the better part of both of us dry.

We stopped for a while and I let the reins hang loosely over Joe's neck while I took in the scene. There were few people on the street and the pavement was glazed and shining like black ice. I was looking up and marvelling at how the red tail-lights of the cars were reflected, caught and then seemed to travel along the overhead trolley lines when I was shaken out my reverie by someone shouting at me from a nearby door-way.

"Help! They robbed me! They robbed me!" He was pointing at two men who were running down the opposite side of the street about half a block away.

I gathered up my reins, dug my spurs into Joe's flanks and we were off like a shot. In a matter of seconds, we had overtaken the slower of the two men and cornered him in a store doorway.

I swung down out of the saddle; he tried to dodge by me but I managed to shove him up against the store's big window while I fumbled through my rain cape to get at my handcuffs. They snagged on the inside of the coat and I had to look down for a second or two to free them.

When I looked up again the man I was holding had pulled out a large butcher knife and was levelling it at my chest.

Just then Joe, who had been standing patiently at my side, took a step forward and nudged the man, pinning him against the window.

The man threw his arms in the air, dropping the knife and screaming, "Okay! Okay! Okay!, Call him off please."

I cuffed the man's arms around a lamppost, swung up on Joe and chased the second man down the centre of Young Street.

He had a gun in his hand and wheeled around once or twice, pointing it at me; it was the first time I had had to draw my own gun but, thankfully, I didn't have to use it because he ducked into an alleyway where we couldn't follow, and he got away.

I caught up with and arrested him about a month later, but that's another story.

Garry Leeson

HORSE GETS HIS MAN

Metro police horse named Joe captured a man yesterday outside a drug store at Alexander St. Constable Garry Leeson heard druggist Leo Gerry cry he'd been held up. Galloping to rescue, Joe pinned one to wall; other got away.

34: Glenspey

Glenspey was not a pretty mare. She was a mousy bay colour with a coarse head, and legs and feet that showed too much of her draft herit-age. The one feature that made her stand out from the rest of the police mounts was her abnormally short tail; the flesh and bone of the actual tail were still intact, but the hairs were very sparse and short.

The older members of the unit claimed that she once sported a very long, thick, luxurious tail and that the cop in charge of her grooming, ig-noring the regulation that police horses should have their tails trimmed off just below the hocks, took great pride in her lengthy locks and went out of his way to encourage their growth. Her tail, in fact, was so long that when she was relaxed it rested on the floor of her stall and that, un-fortunately, proved to be her undoing.

One morning as she lay cuddled down in her bed of straw with her tail tucked under her, a group of boisterous cops from the station next door burst into the stable and startled her. When she leapt to her feet her tail remained pinned under her hind foot and, to quote Robbie Burns, "She left behind her ain grey tail."

Her tail wasn't grey but she sure as hell ripped it off and left most of it lying on the floor. It never completely grew back again, and its absence did nothing to enhance her beauty.

As odd as her appearance was, it was not that alone that made her such a memorable mount. She also had a peculiar habit that I was to learn about during my stay at 56 Division.

I had ridden my young horses quite hard during the first of the week and thought they could use a rest, so I offered to exercise one of the older, regular ones. "You pick someone who needs some exercise," I sug-gested to the senior man, Sy Hawley.

He looked at the other two men present and, after some knowing glances back and forth, an unspoken consensus seemed to be reached. Sy said, "Take old Glenspey, she hasn't been out for a few days. Why don't you take her down to Riverdale Park so you can give her a bit of a run?"

"Sounds good to me," I said as I gathered up my grooming kit and headed for the mare's stall.

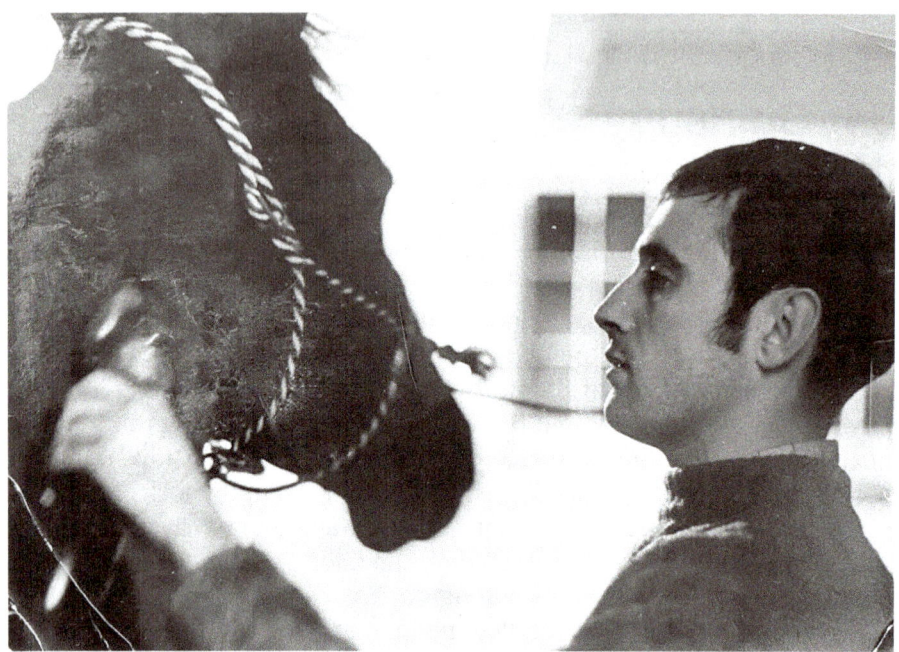

As I brushed away at the old horse, I noticed that the men I had just left were now in a huddle, talking softly to each other, occasionally throwing quick glances in my direction. I didn't make too much out of it. They all had finished half a shift on the street and were about to spend the rest of the day in the stable filling out reports. I figured they were comparing notes.

I got the old horse saddled up and took her out to the yard and, as I swung up onto her back, I noticed that all three men had come to the doorway to see me off, a gesture that seemed uncharacteristically civil of them.

"See you around three o'clock!" one of them shouted as I ambled out of the parking lot.

He must have been mistaken because my shift wasn't over until four thirty and it was only one thirty.

I could see why Glenspey spent so much time standing in the stable. She was totally devoid of energy and ambition and I had to constantly bang away at her sides to get her to trudge along at a walk.

It took about an hour to cover the short distance to the park, but it seemed like forever. Every time I would get her on the verge of a trot she would spy a traffic light about to change and stop on her own and it would take a heroic effort to get her moving again.

"So that's what those buggers were up to," I thought. "They were having a little joke on the hot-shot horse trainer."

I guess I did look quite comical plodding along the busy street on a tailless nag, but if that was the worst they had to dish out I could take it. What the hell, the pay was just the same and I didn't have any deadlines to meet, so I decided to relax and get a good look at the scenery as it, ever so slowly, passed by.

We finally reached Riverdale Park and sidled downhill towards the old zoo. I hadn't been there in years, not since I was a kid in Cabbage Town.

We used to go down frequently to watch the monkeys doing 'it' or to check out the huge Norwegian sewer rats running around the rabbit warren with baby bunnies in their jaws. The place was an outmoded, run-down dump. Thank goodness they later built a new facility and moved the animals to better homes.

However, on the day in question the old zoo still existed and Glenspey and I were slowly making our way to its centre where a sizable crowd was gathered around the compounds that held the larger animals.

I reined the old horse in, dug out my memo book and started making some entries. I had only sat there for a very short time when I began to feel something strange happening beneath me.

The old horse had begun to shiver and was moving her weight restlessly from one foot to another. She threw her head up in the air and her ears began to rotate, scanning around like hairy radar antennas and listening expectantly.

She snorted loudly through her nose once or twice, and was answered by a thunderous trumpeting behind us and some distance away.

We both swung our heads back at the same time and were startled by the sight of a huge elephant hurtling himself toward us. He had a murderous look on his face as, bugling frantically, he charged, stiff legged, toward us with his enormous trunk coiled above his head, ready to slap down anything or anybody that got in his way.

I only had a split second to speculate on the strength of the fence around his enclosure, because Glenspey suddenly went into a wild panic and bolted forward. I had to hang on for dear life.

I had my hands full ,but not with the reins because they were still drooped over her withers, where I had placed them when we stopped. I had a death grip on the pommel of the saddle with one hand and my memo book clutched in the other.

As the old girl took off on automatic pilot, she steadily picked up speed. The crowd parted and the peanut vendors and balloon salesmen dove for cover, scattering bags of nuts and launching a gay profusion of brightly-coloured helium balloons.

Somehow I managed to tuck my memo book in my belt, lean forward and catch hold of the reins as we left the zoo grounds and hit the soft grass of the park, but she motored on undeterred, snorting, farting, and launching divots with her oversized hooves.

I hauled back as hard as I could and shouted, 'Whoa!' several times, but my effort seemed to go unnoticed. She was in fact increasing her speed all the time, and by the time we left the park and hit Broadview Avenue she was going full tilt.

I had the reins in both hands and was pulling so hard that her chin was touching her chest, but still she thundered on, sparks flying when her shoes hit the pavement and foam blowing out of her nostrils.

"Whoa, horse! Whoa, horse whoa, ah—c'mon, horse, whoa!" I shouted, to no avail.

There was one brief respite when the old girl saw a red light at an intersection and screeched to a halt. Even then she danced on the spot, reared, fidgeted, and was generally uncooperative until the light turned to green and she once again took the bit in her mouth and we were off like a shot.

We flew on in the same fashion through several more intersections. Thank God the lights were green and the pedestrians had the good sense to get out of the way.

I thought we were going to hit the pavement as she skidded around the final turn and headed towards the stable, but somehow she managed to keep her footing and stayed in a full canter until she made a sliding stop directly in front of the stable door.

The three guys I had left earlier were now hanging over the lower half of the stable door, and one of them was consulting his watch.

"Two forty- five," he said. "I believe that's a bit of a record."

Then they all started laughing hysterically. They hadn't bothered to tell me that Glenspey and the elephant did not get along and that whenever the elephant started trumpeting, the horse would become so agitated that she would make a beeline for the safety of the stable and nothing in God's world would stop her.

I wasn't the first to be humbled by the tailless horse, and I made sure I wasn't the last. Before I left the division a new man arrived, and he was constantly sounding off about what a great horseman he was. When we all had had enough of his bravado we decided a trip to the zoo was in order.

On this occasion, Glenspey arrived at the stable door twenty minutes before her rider. She had parted company with him before she left the park and he had had to commandeer a trolley to get back to the stable.

He arrived pale, battered and infinitely more humble.

35: Yorkville

If you trotted your horse southeast down Davenport Road from the old stable on New Street, it only took you five minutes to reach Yorkville Avenue. In the early 1960s, the street and its environs had slowly become a haven for a few art galleries and jazz clubs, but as time passed the number of these places increased and were joined by folk music venues, gift shops and coffee houses. All the residences on Yorkville were converted into store fronts and the whole street was transformed into a bohemian village at the very centre of the very conservative city of Toronto.

Every summer night, and most days, the street was filled with huge crowds milling about, going in and out of the clubs and shops, and having a good look at the regulars who had become known as hippies. These were kids who had truly bought into the scene, wandering the streets decked out in their colourful smocks, fringed leather vests, beads and headbands and trying desperately to look cool.

The amount of long hair and beards being sported prompted one the guys on the unit to speculate that the only thing the street didn't have was a good barbershop.

There was always a cacophony of sound as the crowd noise competed with the cries of the street hawkers and the blare of loudspeakers posted outside each of the clubs. The sugary tones of Gordon Lightfoot down at the Riverboat competed with the throbbing backbeat of the music accompanying the go-go girls dancing in the second-floor window of the Myna Bird.

It was like a circus, and hanging over it all was a sweet cloud of marijuana smoke. I think it was this, the blatant use of illegal drugs that caused the police force to focus its attention on the area and launch a couple of raids on the street under the guise of opening it up to allow motor vehicles through. There were plenty of alternative routes in the area and lots of parking; nobody really needed to drive through the street.

Prior to these raids, the men of the mounted unit had a very good rapport with the people of the street; now relations were strained and for the first time I heard the word "Pig" whispered as I rode through.

If I had the choice, I would always ride a mare when I patrolled Yorkville. That way, when some smart-ass said, "Look at the big prick on that horse," he would have some explaining to do.

I didn't give a damn what the so-called hippies did as long as they didn't hurt themselves or anybody else. Of course, occasionally, someone would have a bad acid trip or an overdose, or assault someone who didn't agree with them concerning one of the hot political issues of the day, like keeping troops in Vietnam or abortion on demand, but in general things were strained but manageable.

I knew and was friends with many people who worked and hung out around Yorkville and, although I didn't mention it around the station, I spent quite a bit of my off-duty time around the street myself.

I loved folk music and, after a few beers at Place Pigalle around the corner to gain some courage, I would hit one of the coffee houses and join in the hootnannies. Neither was I immune to the siren call of the go-go girls.

For the most part, I liked the people. Of course, there were a few whom I disliked, but only one whom I detested. His name was Eset Greiber

The street had become a magnet for run-away kids from all over the country, many of them slipping into town to see the Beatles and then staying. The young girls were most at risk. Some of them survived by couch-hopping and working part-time at the coffee houses and clubs; others ended up as sex slaves for petty dope dealers.

Greiber preyed on those girls. Knowing they had little choice, he would offer them food, a flop, and a very small amount of money in exchange for selling flowers for him. I would see these sad, stoned little Lisa Doolittles plying their trade around the area at all hours of the night.

He was a weird-looking fellow, dark and thickset, and with a heavy accent. He was a recent immigrant from Eastern Europe who dressed, formally, in a jacket and tie with a homburg on his head; the good impressions his clothes might have made were negated when you noticed that his trousers were too short and that he wore no shoes or socks, ever!

Greiber might have looked comical, but he had the personality of a viper. He was evil personified, a man who thwarted the law, took illicit advantage of his new country and used every opportunity he could to discredit the police department.

Once when I returned to the station and checked through the photographs in my lost kid file I recognized a picture as being one of the flower girls I had seen on the street earlier that evening. I jumped in my car and headed back to where I had seen her, but she was gone.

When I found and confronted her sleazy boss with the photograph, he denied ever having seen her. Then he took my badge number and complained to headquarters that I was harassing him. I had quite a bit of explaining to do, as policemen, unlike the general public, are considered guilty until proven innocent.

When I learned that I was being transferred to the Exhibition Grounds to act as horse trainer and riding instructor, I knew that I was going to miss the excitement of Yorkville, but I sure wasn't going miss Greiber.

I had one last evening shift to spend on the street, and I spent most of it enjoying the sights and saying goodbye to some of the regulars.

It was almost time to head back to the stables and I was making some final entries in my memo book when I noticed a crowd gathering at the intersection where Hazelton Avenue meets Yorkville. I couldn't see what was going on from where I was, so I put my book away and gave old Major a dig in the ribs and pointed him towards the commotion.

I leaned forward in anticipation of the surge of power that was to follow, but I had forgotten which horse I was on, and there was no hurrying old Major. He just took his time ambling over to the scene with me kicking away at his sides and clucking encouragement.

We arrived at the corner to find a denser pocket of the already-crowded street gathered around a yellow cab parked by the curb with its rear passenger door swung open over the sidewalk. An older man was confronting one of the flower girls. He had hold of her basket of roses and they were engaged in a gentle tug of war.

A woman who looked to be the same age as the man stood between him and the girl, with her arms stretched out and her hands resting on each of their shoulders. She seemed to be pleading with them as she turned to face first one and then the other.

I climbed down off of Major and he stood quietly while I made my way over to the kerfuffle to see what was going on.

The woman explained through her tears that the flower girl, one I had never seen before, was their daughter. She had disappeared from their farm near Orangeville, north of Toronto, several months earlier and they had just found her, but she wouldn't listen to reason and come home with them.

"How old is she?" I asked.

"She's only fourteen" the woman wailed.

I have a sister, Brenda, who was about the same age as this girl at the time and living with my parents on a farm north of the city I pictured my parents trying to deal with a situation like this and it didn't take me long to make up my mind whose side I was on.

I took the basket from between the father and daughter and, keeping the girl in view out of the corner of my eye, turned to her father and said. "I know how these kids think. Why don't you and your wife wait in the cab while I see if I can convince her?"

Obviously stoned, the girl was looking frantically around for an escape route, so I grabbed her firmly by the shoulder with my free hand, leaned in close and whispered in her ear, "Listen, you little bitch, you get in that cab before I kick your ass. Don't say a word or I'll have you down to the station so fast it will make your head spin."

With that I shoved her into the back of the cab and into her parents' arms. I slammed the door shut, and as the cab sped away I was feeling pretty smug and self-satisfied as I turned to see how my horse was making out in my absence.

That's when I realized that I still had the basket of roses in my hand. Major noticed them immediately and was chewing away on one of the blossoms before I could swing the basket out of his reach.

"Stop that!" I said while I held the basket even further away as he edged forward, looking for seconds.

What to do? What to do? It was getting late, I had to get going but I couldn't just dump the basket. I had just explained my way out of my last scrape with the basket's owner and I didn't want to start a new one.

There was nothing for it. I got one of the women who had been patting Major to hold the basket of flowers while I mounted up. She handed me the basket and I ran my left arm through the arch of the handle and then grabbed my reins in the same hand.

I settled myself into the saddle and adjusted the basket into a comfortable position, then set off through the crowd, trying to be as inconspicuous as possible.

Who was I kidding? We hadn't gone ten feet before the boos, hoots and jeers started. Someone yelled out, the inevitable, "Look at the big prick on that horse!" and that is when I lost it.

I could hear the strains of a song drifting down from a second story window: "Now if you're going to San Francisco..." I think that's what inspired me,

I took a rose from the basket and shoved the stem under my hat band so that the flower looked to be resting on my ear. Then, while moving forward, I started tossing flowers left and right into the crowd.

The effect was immediate. The hoots and jeers turned to clapping and cheers and everyone seemed to be smiling and laughing.

When I reached Avenue Road, Greiber was standing bare footed, on the corner, glaring up at me;

I took the basket into my free hand and tossed it down to him and then, after giving him the finger, I rode off into the sunset.

36:The raccoon

The sun was already setting as I hurried my horse down the steep road to the Central Don Park in North Toronto. In the short time it took to go down the hill, I was transported from the busy city streets to a tranquil country setting where there was no trace of the city.

When it reaches the valley floor, the road leads over a small bridge that crosses the Don River and then on to the Metropolitan Toronto Police Mounted Unit Headquarters. The headquarters had barns and stables and two houses that once made up the farm of a private estate.

Two men stood at the entrance of the police stable. One was my Sergeant, and the other was the Superintendent of the Park. They were having a heated conversation and only looked up when my horse's metal shoes left the soft turf and hit the cobblestone in front of the building.

The Sergeant pulled his pipe out and grunted, "Good, you're here. Put your horse away. We've got a job for you."

By the time I had unsaddled my horse, fed and watered him and made my way back to the waiting men, the sun had sunk further behind the rim of the valley, leaving that glorious red that only city pollution can produce. Visibility was minimal.

Between puffs on his pipe, the Sergeant laid out my assignment. Apparently the Park's Superintendent, who lived in a cottage just out of sight of where we stood, had noticed a raccoon high in one of the stately elms that shaded his house. It seemed that the raccoon was acting strangely—aggressive and vicious—unusual for these semi-tame park animals. There had been a rabies scare recently and there was no sense taking any chances.

"Take your pistol over there and humanely destroy that animal," came the directive. "And here's a feed bag to bring him back in. Be quick about it because it's getting dark."

The streetlights had just come on as the two men turned their backs on me and continued their conversation.

I felt the weight of my holster to make sure that my trusty, if rusty, 32-calibre Colt was at my side, and then proceeded toward the crime scene. I had had to check my gun because I hadn't had much occasion to use it and, frankly, wasn't very good with it.

As my fingers ran through my ammunition pouch, I was relieved to find several extra bullets in there. Thank God I had replaced them after wasting so many shots while trying to bag a pheasant during a particularly boring afternoon patrol in Mount Pleasant Cemetery a month or so earlier.

I don't know what had possessed me. I don't like hunting or killing creatures and was relieved when I had come to my senses before I did hit the pheasant.

Now here I was again, this time being sent as executioner of a poor, distressed animal.

I hoped that the raccoon had moved on to another part of the park, but as I approached the base of the tree, I could hear him hissing and snarling with that particular rattle that is peculiar to raccoons. He was still there.

There was enough light from the nearby yard lamp to make out his furry shape and bright eyes. His white gnashing teeth were also visible, but worst of all, I could detect a cascade of white foam drooling down over his lower jaw, a sure sign of distemper or rabies.

"Well, there's nothing for it, he's just going to have to go," I said to myself.

I drew my pistol and assumed the two-handed stance I had been

140

taught at the Police College. One quick, accurate shot should do it. With my arms stretched full length, I sighted along the barrel and decided to put a round between his eyes and end the thing quickly.

Who was I kidding? When we took firearms training, I was the worst in the class. I am convinced that the only way that I passed target practice was because some of the shots from the other cadets training with me strayed onto respectable spots on my target. I had the bad habit of wincing and closing my eyes in anticipation of the bang—sort of a "now you see it, now you don't" technique that was hard to overcome.

I hoped this little bugger was close enough that I might be able to do the deed swiftly and successfully.

I resumed my firing stance, cocked my revolver and let fly in his general direction.

My first shot was well-planned because it trimmed off a large, leafy branch about three feet above his head. This, of course, allowed more light onto the scene and made my target more visible.

"Now you're for it," I thought, as I fired my second shot and was pleased to see that it struck the huge tree about two feet to his right.

It startled the now really pissed off raccoon into turning and facing me full on, presenting a much better target area. I emptied all six chambers of my gun in this fashion without really approaching his immediate vicinity. I was also making quite a lot of noise

I reloaded sheepishly, thankful again for the extra bullets in my pouch.

Again, I assumed the position, ready to restart the barrage. As I squeezed the trigger, the gun sounded a dull 'pop' and I could actually see the bullet leave the end of the barrel and arch to the ground about six feet in front of me. It was a dud.

As I looked up into the tree I could tell that the raccoon was losing all respect for me. In fact, he was climbing down the trunk with his whole body shaking in a maddened tremor.

He was much closer now, so I fired off three shots in rapid succession. He was suddenly very still as he clung to the tree and I breathed a sigh of relief.

I blew the smoke off the end of my pistol and put it in my holster. I grabbed the bag in anticipation of his fall from the tree, but as I was straightening up I heard his mad snarling resume. I had totally missed yet again, and he had only been playing possum, or raccoon as the case may be, and now he was coming for me.

My second to last shot went wild, but as he was about to bite the barrel of my gun, I got off the headshot that I had originally intended. He departed the world in a quick, almost painless fashion, and as I stuffed him in the bag and looked at my watch, I realized that I had been at least half an hour bagging my little friend.

It was dark as I walked the short distance back to the stable, where my Sergeant and the superintendent waited. The Sergeant looked from the Super to me and, slowly removing his pipe from his mouth, asked, "Did that raccoon have a gun, too?"

37: I hate bagpipes

I hate bagpipes,

I didn't always hate them, Prior to 1967 I merely disliked them, but during the spring and summer of that year, when I was exposed to them continually, hour after hour, day after day, I developed a real, lifelong abhorrence.

Inspector Johnson was training his first musical ride with the mounted unit and had enlisted the Metropolitan Toronto Police Pipe Band to provide the music. Not such a bad idea on the surface. The band was steeped in tradition and had a lot of eye appeal, but I had my reservations. Recently, I had ridden in a troupe in front of them, leading the

Santa Claus Parade, and the experience had left a bad taste in my mouth.

Granted their musicianship, as that of pipers goes, was probably very good. There was no doubt that the crowds that lined both sides of the street were enthused by the sight and sound of them, particularly the older guys wearing tam-o-shanters; however, the emotions they stirred in me were quite different.

I was riding King and he seemed equally irked by the proximity of the band as they followed us down the street. They made him nervous and he danced, pranced, threw his head, and blew foam out of his mouth and nostrils.

Maybe the crowd thought he was dancing in time to the music, but Big Ed, who was riding old Major and leading the parade in front of us knew better and kept looking back at me with an evil look of disapproval, finally shouting at me, "Use two hands on that horse, Leeson!"

It was embarrassing as hell, I had complete control of the animal, he only appeared to be about to bolt and run amok through the throngs of tiny tots sitting on the curbs. It wasn't my fault, it was that damned pipe band.

Every time I looked over my shoulder I could see the drum major, a huge, barrel-chested bugger in a Busby, strutting along, tossing his mace in the air and getting uncomfortably close to our horses' rear ends. He was followed by thirty or so kilted giants, squeezing away at their bagpipes and blowing, red-faced, into something that looked like the stem of a hookah.

And the drums, Oh, the drums! How could anyone fail to be moved by the rhythmic roll of the snares and the throb of the big bass drum? I know I was moved—about three feet in the air. Every time the bass drummer whacked his infernal instrument to start yet another monotonous Scottish reel, King would buck and fire me momentarily up and out of the saddle.

The goof playing the huge drum was obviously aware of the effect he was having on King and me, as he swaggered along with a smirk on his face, kilt swaying and decked out in bearskins and the pelts of other endangered species.

I had heard that you didn't need a great deal of talent or brains to play the bass drum, just be able to walk and chew gum at the same time. This guy barely met the minimal criteria and deserved a good kick in the sporran.

King and I finished the parade intact but, thanks to the pipe band, we had not made a very good impression.

Understandably, it was with a certain amount of trepidation that I joined the rest of the crew on a Monday morning and started rehearsing for the musical ride. I knew the pipe band would be present and participating, but the total duration of the ride was only going to be about thirty minutes and I was certain that I could put up with the band's caterwauling for that short period of time. Besides I would be riding Blackie, a young horse I had just broken and trained, and he was nothing like the hot-headed King.

The first rehearsal with the band went well, with all the horses behaving despite the bass drummers attempt to stir them up; Blackie was exceptionally good. It was as if he was born to that kind of job.

When the hour or so was up and we all took a break, I thought that we were through for the day. I hadn't allowed for Big Ed's insistence on perfection. He had Sergeant Lewis, who was now in charge of the musical ride; keep us at it all day long.

And it continued that way, day after day, for weeks on end, with the horses trotting in circles and the sound of the pipes and drums echoing off the rafters of the coliseum. We practised the same routine over and over 'til the horses became so familiar with it that they could make all the moves on their own, as they often did when one of the riders fell off.

But oh, that God-awful noise! It never stopped, even when we stopped to rest and Sergeant Lewis said, "Smoke em if you got em." The pipers would take the opportunity to practice their individual parts, thirty pipers wailing away at thirty different tunes at the same time. It was an acoustic nightmare.

Blackie and I could edge away from the guys who were smoking, but there was no escaping the din of those pipes. I understood now why the Germans during WWI referred to the kilted Scots as "The ladies from Hades."

I wasn't the only horseman who was being driven mad by the pipes. It was during that period that I first heard the classic bagpipe jokes. I take no credit for coming up with them, but I am in complete agreement with the sentiments they express.

Q. What is the definition of a gentleman?
A. Someone who can play the bagpipes but doesn't.

Did you hear about man who left his car to do some shopping? He panicked when he realized that he had left the vehicle unlocked with his very valuable bagpipes lying in plain view on the back seat. When he rushed back to the car and looked in, there were two sets of pipes on the seat.

Once you got those cursed instruments out of their hands, the members of the band turned out to be a great bunch of fun-loving guys and I really enjoyed their company when we celebrated after our performances. The most memorable of these celebrations occurred in 1967, at the conclusion of the last musical ride we did after a week's run at the Canadian National Exhibition.

38: Metro meets the Mounties

During the summer of 2005 I was playing my trumpet in a community band, Kings County Concert Band, and it fell to me to make the arrangements for the group to accompany the R.C.M.P. Musical Ride at the fair grounds at Amherst Nova Scotia.

All the band members were really excited about the gig so I thought it would be neat if we could be photographed with the Mounties and have a souvenir of the event. I contacted the Ride's advance team and they assured me that Mounties would be delighted to pose with us after the performance.

I hired a local photographer to take the picture and we all looked forward to playing for the huge crowd and then getting our picture taken with these icons of the Great White North.

I decided to have one last meeting with the Sergeant in charge to go over the details so that we wouldn't take any more of their time than was necessary. That's when he dropped the bomb.

"I'm sorry!" he said. "There isn't going to be any picture. We reserve that privilege for amateur groups and your band is professional."

What the hell could he be talking about? I was astounded and a little bit flattered.

"The fair management tells me that your group was paid to be here," he continued with his chin jutting skyward.

That's when I lost it, I did remember that the fair committee had given us a small stipend to help with gas for the crowded vehicles we came in, but it wasn't very much. I made some quick mental calculations and then explained to the crusty Mountie that our pay for the two days we devoted to the performance netted each of the band members approximately forty-nine cents.

He could see that my face was getting nearly as red as his tunic and decided to acquiesce. We would get our picture, but as I walked away from him my mind drifted back to a time many years previous when I had met and dealt with an R.C.M.P. sergeant. just like him. I guess it's all right to tell this story now since most of the participants have by now retired, died or simply wouldn't give a damn.

Because it was Centennial Year, the R.C.M.P. were also performing their musical ride at the C.N.E. There wasn't much interaction between them and the members of the Toronto mounted unit; we were stabled in our own partitioned-off area on the first floor of the Horse Palace and the Mounties were up on the second floor at the opposite end of the building.

We wandered up to say hello to them, but they were not very receptive. Although we were all policemen and were involved in musical rides, we didn't seem to have anything else in common.

They were a highly-regimented outfit, always in uniform even when they were mucking out the stalls. They marched in step everywhere they went and there always seemed to be a sergeant around watching their every move.

Our group was always turned out well when we performed, but in between rides or when we were off duty we kicked around in blue jeans and cowboy boots and pretty well did as we pleased. The Mounties were never off duty and they never seemed to be having any fun.

We found out through the grapevine that they had been told by their Inspector not to mix with our group. Most of us didn't care because, from what we had seen of them, they appeared to be a bunch of pompous, over-disciplined stick-in-the-muds, not worthy of our attention.

Near the end of the week, Inspector Johnson got wind of the restrictions his counterpart on the R.C.M.P. had put on his men and decided to confront him about the obvious insult. I wasn't there to see it but I can imagine the look on the Mountie's face with Big Ed towering over him, looking even taller than his six foot four in his white bobby helmet, as he taught him some manners.

He must have been convincing because, shortly after, we got word that the members of the R.C.M.P. musical ride would be joining us for a little get-together at the conclusion of our shows.

It was our custom to keep a small stock of alcoholic beverages waiting for us to wash down the tan bark dust at the end of our rides. Normally it was a BYOB arrangement; we had been cautioned not to offer any to the Mounties but, for some reason, although I'm sure we all intended to comply with the warning, we all showed up with extra beer and bottles of the hard stuff.

Since all of this happened without much planning or consultation, the cache of booze, before we set upon it, was a trifle excessive. There was a hell of a lot of it!

On the last night, the boys from the Toronto unit and the band members got a bit of a head start on the festivities. We were all changed out of our uniforms, reclining on our tack boxes with cold ones in our hands, waiting for the Mounties. It was getting late and we were wondering if they had changed their minds and weren't coming.

Then we heard the sound of thirty pairs of boots hitting the stable pavement in unison. On they came down the aisle in our direction, marching two by two, arms swinging and in perfect step. They were all wearing their full summer street uniform, complete with Stetsons.

Their Sergeant broke off and hup-hupped them through the tack room door and then halted the troop in the centre. Their Inspector followed them in and, after he gave the Sergeant a nod, they were all dismissed, and the group spread out among our guys and the band members.

The Mounties started shaking hands and making some formal attempts at conversation, but you could tell that they were nervous and uptight.

When I offered the one closest to me a beer, he almost had a heart attack.

"No, no, no!" he whispered, rolling his eyes and glancing over his shoulder in the direction of his sergeant.

I could see why: this sergeant had everybody intimidated. He was the biggest man in the room; he even had an inch or two on Big Ed. He looked to be a fit two hundred and thirty pounder, with the physique of a weight lifter and the permanent sneer of a drill instructor.

He was a handsome bugger with Aryan features, blue eyes and short blonde hair showing below the brim of his Stetson. Hitler would have loved him.

Inspector Johnson had greeted the Mountie Inspector as soon as he entered the room and now he had his arm around his shoulder, leading him over to a makeshift bar we had constructed. I watched as he poured two drinks and handed one to the Mountie, who took it but then, shaking his head from side to side, promptly placed it back down on the bar.

A bit of animated conversation ensued, but the glass remained on the bar. It was looking as if the Mountie had won the day and was not about to take a drink but then Big Ed made a masterful manoeuvre.

"Gentlemen, can I have your attention!" he shouted over the noise of the room, "This is Canada's centennial year and, on behalf of the Metropolitan Toronto Police and the R.C.M.P. I would like to propose a toast to

Queen and Country."

The Mountie Inspector looked like he wanted to run out of the room, but he reluctantly picked up the glass and, after he nodded his approval, his whole contingent followed suit, grabbing the bottles and glasses eagerly proffered by our guys and the members of the band.

It was a lingering toast, not your customary sip, and when that one was over, certain other dignitaries were remembered and subsequent toasts made until finally we were all left on our own to, individually, toast whomever we chose as often as we wanted.

I guess the Mountie Inspector figured, "What the hell. In for a penny, in for a pound," because he spent the next hour or so in conversation with Big Ed and looking the other way.

His big lantern-jawed Sergeant wasn't too impressed with what was going on and kept looking in his Ispector's direction, hoping for the order to shut things down. But that order never came, so he just stood in a corner, nursing his original drink and scanning the room with a sour look on his face.

A relaxed atmosphere settled over the gathering and the tension the young Mounties had displayed earlier was all but gone; ties were removed, and collars opened. Most of the brown Stetsons were off their closely-shorn heads and hooked over saddle cantles or bridle racks.

About halfway through the evening, the R.C.M.P. Inspector received an urgent message delivered by one of our policewomen. He had to return to his hotel, so Big Ed volunteered to drive him.

On his way out he slurred some final instructions to his Sergeant. "Just stay a little longer then wrap things up."

As the two inspectors made their way through the stable on their way to Big Ed's car, they had to pass a large pile of baled straw. When they got to the far side of it they happened on a young Mountie who had borrowed a guitar from one our guys and was sitting on a bale, serenading an equally young Metro policewoman who was perched near the top of the pile. Most of the young man's uniform had been discarded; he still had his britches and boots, but he was down to his t-shirt and had his tie around his head like a bandana.

The Mountie Inspector instinctively started to admonish him but ,before he could speak, Big Ed steered him away and hustling him over to his car, muttered in his ear, "By God, that boy has a good voice!"

In the absence of the inspectors and in spite of the Mountie Sergeant's presence, the party took a turn for the worse.

First one of the Mounties came riding into the room on old Roy, bareback, with a Metro policewoman sitting sidesaddle behind him. When Roy stopped suddenly, she lost her balance and fell over backwards and into the arms of a batch of Mounties who caught her, then started passing her from one to the other across the room.

She was laughing hysterically, and no one was paying much attention to the direction in which she was being shuttled. When her final destination turned out to be the arms of the big Sergeant over in the corner, it was obvious that he was not amused.

As he put her down, brushed off the front of his uniform and straightened his hat, I could tell that he was about to call a halt to the proceedings. I quickly conferred with a couple of my close associates and we devised a plan to distract him. It was something we had done many times before, so I trusted my friends to do the groundwork while I left the room to prepare myself.

The Sergeant had already started to gather his men around him as my friends approached him. They had all heard him bragging about his prowess in the gym, so they knew he was a prime candidate for what they were about to propose.

Before he could speak to his men, one of my conspirators in a very loud voice put the question to him. "Excuse me, Sergeant. I was wondering, who would you say was the strongest man in your outfit?"

With a haughty look on his face that suggested that the answer should be obvious, he sneered, "I guess that would be me."

Our man continued, "Why don't we have a test of strength between your strongest man, which is you, and the strongest man in our unit?"

The big Mountie did a quick scan of the room, taking in our spindly arms and beer bellies, then uttered a confident, "Why not?"

You could tell that he wanted to inflict some punishment on the group that had so shamelessly undermined all of his discipline.

My friends explained the rules. They said it was a traditional cavalry contest to test the strength of a trooper's neck muscles. "You will lie spread-eagled on the floor, face down, bracing yourself in any manner you choose. Your opponent will kneel beside you with his hands behind his back and, using only his head, attempt to roll you over. If he is successful, the contest is over. If he fails to roll you over you, will get the opportunity to address him in the same manner."

"Why me first?" he asked.

"Tradition!" my buddies chorused.

The answer didn't really seem to satisfy him, but just then I came prancing into the circle that had been cleared in the centre of the room. I was bare-chested, one hundred and forty pounds soaking wet and, as I danced around playing to the crowd, shadow boxing and humming the theme from Rocky, my big opponent stammered, "What is this a joke?"

"No Joke," one of my friends shot back, "He may look puny, but he has incredibly strong neck muscles, so you better brace yourself."

"This is ridiculous," said the big Mountie "But we may as well get it over with so we can get out of here."

He started to crouch down, but he was stopped by one of our men who made his way to the centre of the circle with a partial bottle of Southern Comfort in his hand.

"What say we make this contest interesting?" he said, "The loser has to finish this bottle off in no more than three snorts."

The crowd cheered unanimous approval and I said modestly, "I really like Southern Comfort."

"Whatever," said the big Sergeant. "Let's get on with it."

He dropped to the floor and did series of pushups to warm up and then assumed the position.

I dropped to my knees near the half-way point of his body. He looked even bigger from this perspective.

He was looking back and over his shoulder at me, so I crossed myself to emphasize the seriousness of the occasion then placed my hands behind my back.

I gave him a couple of tentative test nudges with the top of my head, and each time I did he tensed up, pressing down on his wide-spread arms and legs till his torso lifted clear of the ground and every muscle was bulging and defined. Clearly I had my work cut out for me.

I touched his flank with my head a couple of more times, and that's when he made the mistake of relaxing for a split second and I was able to deliver the *coup de grace*.

With the speed of a striking cobra, I lunged forward and sunk my teeth into the softest part of his ass and bit down as hard as I could.

He let out a stifled scream and immediately flipped over onto his back. He made a grab for me with a murderous look on his face, but I managed to slip away and get to my feet before he could do any real damage.

He got up and moved toward me, shaking his clenched fists, but by then the whole room had broken into peals of laughter and he had second thoughts and backed off.

I guess he didn't want his crew to think he was a bad sport. Without saying another word, he snatched the bottle of Southern Comfort out of my friend's hand and drank it down, in two long gulps. "Who needs three swallows?" he said as he handed the empty bottle back to my friend, as if his prowess in this regard had to some extent restored a bit of his dignity.

He spent the next few minutes with a group of his trainees gathered around him, explaining why, because of his size, he was not affected by alcohol in the same way that a smaller, less muscular type would be. Then he sat down on a tack box and promptly passed out.

The guys from our unit took him out to the stable and bedded him down in a box stall with old Major. The last I saw of him, he was mumbling something that sounded like pillow talk and smiling serenely while Major nuzzled his neck and chest and rooted at his breast pockets, looking for treats.

In the total absence of any authority figure of consequence, the boys really let their hair down and things took a further turn for the worse. It was well past closing time at the exhibition, so the party spread out into the corridors of the Horse Palace. An impromptu game of Donkey Baseball was organized in the riding ring and more than the bases were loaded.

Some of the Mounties were taking bagpipe lessons from the band members and insisting on borrowing their kilts while doing it; they had been told that proper protocol dictated that nothing was to be worn under the garments and they weren't shy about bending over periodically and displaying their adherence to the rules.

One man was marching up and down the pavement outside the stable wearing a kilt, tall riding boots with spurs, a Mountie Stetson and carrying a bamboo lance. It was difficult to tell exactly which outfit he was with.

Another kilted band member was indulging in his own version of the highland games, he had a stack of about a dozen Mountie hats and he was tossing them like Frizbees, trying to get them onto the ramp of the Gardiner Expressway. He wasn't very successful because I could see several of the pointy topped hats littering the parking lot directly in front of him.

It was at this juncture that I decided that it was time for me to leave the party. The decision may not have been entirely mine because I remember somebody holding onto my ear and guiding me out. Anyway, I didn't want to be around when the big Mountie Sergeant. woke up.

I had it from reliable sources that the party continued for some time after I left and even had a change of venue for its finale. The papers carried a story the following day concerning a group of young Mounties and an unspecified of number Metro Toronto policewomen caught playing nude water polo in the pool at the Lakeshore Motel.

I was at the Horse Palace the following day to watch the Mounties ship out. They seemed cool and stand-offish. An official directive had been issued: "Under no circumstances will any member of the R.C.M.P. musical ride ever again fraternize with members of The Metropolitan Toronto Police Mounted Unit."

It may not be on the books, but I believe the order still stands.

39: Donny

I had a look at some old service records recently and was pleased to see that Warren Pollard, a guy I worked with at 33 Division in Scarborough had been promoted to the rank of Sergeant before he retired. I liked Warren. He was a real straight shooter and, while some of us on the mounted unit were naughty rascals at times, he was always above-board and shied away from our high-jinks.

He was an athlete and represented our Department in competitions with other police forces across Canada and the U.S. He had the metabolism of a runner, right off the mark when he needed to be but laid back and low keyed the rest of the time. It was pretty hard to get him excited or nervous.

I mention all this to emphasize how unusual and unlike him it was the one time, in the early winter of 1969, that I saw him really lose it, and, to tell the truth, it was entirely my fault.

It all started one afternoon as I was riding up Birchmount Avenue, returning to the stable for lunch. As we approached the intersection at Lawrence Avenue my horse stopped suddenly. I hadn't noticed the traffic light changing to red, but he did.

While we waited for the light to change to green, a strange-looking young man stepped down off the curb and started patting my horse's neck and muzzle. Wwhat he was doing wasn't unusual, it happened all the time, but the weird appearance of the man himself caught my attention.

It was the end of a long, hot summer and, whereas everybody in the crowd that he had stepped out of was sporting a dark tan, his complexion was a pasty pallor; and that, together with his mop of messy white-blond hair, gave him the appearance of an albino. His moist, red, bulbous lips seemed to reinforce this impression and only his very dark brown eyes discounted it. His mouth was perpetually wide open with the widely-spaced teeth of both the upper and lower jaw were constantly exposed; a sort of Quasimodo sans the hump.

"Nice horse," he said looking up at me with eyes that seemed to suggest that 'the lights were on, but nobody was home'.

I nodded agreement and he continued, "I know all about horses, I worked at a stable looking after them."

"That's nice," I said as the light changed to green and my horse fidgeted forward, telling me it was time to move on.

That's when he said something that sparked my attention, "I've been working for Christilot Hanson, taking care of her horses."

"Really? I said, immediately reining my horse up and over the sidewalk, stopping him on a grassy patch beside the bus shelter. The strange guy shuffled along with me and resumed caressing the horse as soon as we stopped.

I had to know more. Ms. Hanson was currently the Canadian Dressage champion and enjoying quite a bit of international fame. More to the point, she was a really attractive woman. I had watched her riding at the Royal Winter Fair, and I was impressed with more than her riding skills.

"So, what's your name" I asked the strange man, who by now had my horse's mouth open and was checking his teeth.

"My name is Donald Jones," he replied very formally, but then, shyly looking down at his feet, said, "But you can call me Donny."

After introducing myself, I started to pump him for information. First I wanted to be sure that he wasn't putting me on, so I hit him with, "Tell me, Donny, where did you work when you were taking care of Christilot's horses?"

He described the location, and he was right on the mark, I had driven by her stable and knew where it was.

"So, what did you do there?" I continued and Donny described all the jobs he had done, mucking out stalls, grooming horses, cleaning tack, etc.

"What was Christalot like to work for?" I asked.

"Oh, okay, I guess."

I hit him with a few more inquires, then finished up by asking why he wasn't working there anymore.

At that he bristled, tensed up, and sputtered out a very firm, "I don't want to talk about that!"

I assumed from his reaction that he was probably the victim of some snobbery; after all, he wasn't the coolest-looking item to have hanging around a fancy stable. So I let the matter drop. "Catch you later," I said, and made an attempt to leave.

But Donny stepped in front of my horse and, looking up at me with sad, imploring eyes, said, "Wait! I could look after your horses. Really, I could,"

"Thanks Donny," I replied, "but we look after our own horses"

"Yeah, but I could help. I'd work hard, I really would."

The man was pathetic, and his pleas were beginning to draw the attention of the crowd gathered around the bus shelter, so I said the only thing I could think of. "Look, Donny, we don't hire civilians, but I'm sure it would be all right for you to come and visit the stables sometime. We often did tours for the public so it wouldn't be a big deal."

"Oh good, that's good," he said. "Can I come now?"

When I told him that I didn't think that we could do it right away he became very upset and agitated, and as I scanned the crowd around us I could tell by their expressions that they thought I was being cruel.

So I relented and, leaning down and talking softly, said, "Okay, Donny. The stable is just around the corner. I'll see you there in a few minutes."

I barely had time to put my horse away when I heard him knocking. I slung my saddle onto the cleaning rack and headed to the main stable entrance.

The top half of the door was all window, and as I approached it I had a really good look at Donny for the first time. His head and upper torso were framed in the safety glass and the embedded wire was casting a strange pattern on his pasty face. The sprint over from the bus stop had caused his already dishevelled hair to explode into a Medusa-like coif, and he stood there with his eyes darting right and left, trying to get a glimpse inside.

As I pulled the door open and greeted him I would not have been surprised if he had said, "Trick or treat."

I ushered him in and over to where the horses were tied in their standing stalls, and watched as he walked slowly up and down the aisle, looking at the horses. He was obviously enjoying the experience and I thought I saw a hint of a smile as the horses swung their heads around to see their strange admirer.

I let him linger awhile while I got out my shovel and broom and opened the trap door to the manure pit that was in the floor at the rear of the stable. Quite a large offering of glistening horse droppings had accumulated while I was out on patrol and I wanted to clean them up before the horses and I had our supper.

I reached for the shovel that I had left leaning on the wall, but Donny beat me to it, clutching the handle with a weird, possessive look on his face. He startled me, and I instinctively felt for my gun. For a moment I thought he was about to hit me with the shovel; instead, while I watched dumbfounded, he set about scooping up the manure and shovelling it down the dung hole. Then he grabbed the broom and sweeping the floor and tidying up, all this without ever uttering a word.

When he finished, he followed me around the corner and into the tack room, and stood watching while I filled a bucket with warm water and got out my amber bar of saddle soap, wipe rags and can of Brasso. I only had time to run a wet rag up the length of one stirrup leather before Donny crept up close behind me and stood looking over my shoulder.

I continued cleaning my saddle for a while, but I wasn't that comfortable with his drooling and heavy breathing, so I handed him the rag and stepped back to watch.

He seemed to know what he was up to and he was going at it with more energy or enthusiasm than I ever could, so I left him to it and retired to the lunchroom.

From where I sat, looking through the door with my feet up, nibbling away at my baloney sandwiches, I could see Donny working away at my complete set of tack. There was no doubt about it; he was good, The only time he stopped scrubbing and polishing was when one of the horses would lift its tail and plop another offering onto the floor. Each time he would immediately rush into the stable, scoop it up and shovel it down the hole; he actually looked disappointed once when he rushed into the stable only to find that one of the horses had farted a false alarm.

I have to admit that I was impressed and sat for some time pondering the possibilities.

My thoughts were interrupted by the sound of Warren Pollard's horse's hooves clattering on the cobbles outside the stable. This was going to take some explaining.

Warren didn't notice Donny as he hustled his horse into the stable and removed the saddle and bridle; he wasn't aware of his presence until he almost bumped into him going into the tack room and was so startled by his appearance that he dropped his saddle. Fortunately, I was there to stay his hand as he went for his gun.

"Who the hell is that?" he stammered as I took his arm and guided him into the lunchroom, leaving Donny to pick up his saddle.

It took quite a while for me to get Warren caught up with what had been happening, and by the time I was done, Donny was nearly finished cleaning Warren's kit as well.

We both agreed that there was no point in stopping him now, so we put on the kettle and settled down to enjoy a leisurely lunch.

When he had finished in the tack room, Donny found our currycombs and brushes and set about grooming the horses. I decided that a nap was in order, and Warren, who was always up for a snooze, decided to join me.

When quitting time rolled around and it was time to go home, the stable, tack and horses were looking the best we had ever seen them.

We both escorted Donny to the stable door, thanking him profusely for his good work with Warren looking thankful that the day and Donny's presence in the stable was finally over.

That's why Warren was so upset when Donny asked if he could come back the following day and I said, "Sure!"

He slammed the door shut, almost hitting Donny in the rear end, and started shouting, "Are you out of your mind? We can't have that crazy bastard hanging around here. What if the Sergeant finds out?"

"Look, Warren," I replied in a comforting tone, "I don't know about you, but I really like police work and patrolling on the horses, but what I don't like is coming back to this stable and working like a galley slave. And why should we when this young fellow wants nothing more than spend his time here doing the things that I, and I'm sure you, dislike so much? I think we should give it a try. What have we got to lose?"

"What have we got to lose?" he sputtered. "Just our jobs you, nitwit."

"Take it easy, take it easy! "I shot back at him, "I've thought this out and I have a plan. Here's what we do: you know when you suggest some unreasonable chore for your wife to do and she gets miffed and sarcastically says, 'Okay, I'll get the maid to do that'? Well, from now on, whenever Sergeant Lewis comes along and orders us to do any maintenance, we just laugh and say, 'Okay, I'll get Donny to do that right away,' as if he was an imaginary maid. That way if we get caught in the future we can implicate the Sergeant by saying, "Gosh, we've been telling you about Donny for ages now."

I don't think Warren really bought into the plan, but the thought of all those extra hours of relaxation were too much for him to resist, so he reluctantly agreed, and Donny began his regular visits.

As time went on, the other mounted guys stationed with us joined into the arrangement and everybody seemed happy, particularly Donny. There were some narrow escapes when Sergeant Lewis made unscheduled visits and we had to shove Donny down the manure hole to hide him; he didn't seem to mind, and when we retrieved him he was always smelly but happy.

One afternoon, we got a surprise visit from a teacher and her elementary school class. It was on the calendar, but we hadn't noticed. Donny had just recently been stuffed in the manure bin and we didn't have the heart to make him do it again so soon, so instead we dressed him up in a spare uniform, complete with hat, badge and Sam Browne. He was quite a sight as he stood rigidly at attention, beaming and drooling, with his long frizzy blonde hair sticking out from under his too small hat.

Of course, we introduced him to the teacher as Constable Jones and enjoyed her reaction so much that we made him a regular feature on all the school tours. Nobody enjoyed it more than Donny.

By the time winter set in, our secret stable man had turned into a fixture and was happily taking on more and more of the work around the place. Recently he had even been asking to stay in the stable while we went out on patrol so that he could finish off whatever he was working on.

As these requests became more frequent, as ungrateful as it might seem, our police instincts kicked in and we began to be suspicious about what he might be up to when he was alone in the stable.

One afternoon, when Warren and I were working together, we decided it was time to check up on Donny. The weather was bad, so instead of taking the horses out we decided to patrol in our van.

We made a big show of saying goodbye to Donny, explaining that we would be patrolling the far side of the division and telling him to make sure that he watered the horses one last time before he left.

We drove off, but only went a short distance, parked the van out of sight, and skulked back to the rear of the stable. A metal fire escape led up to a fire door with a large window in it that opened into the stable area. We climbed silently up to the door and peered through the window.

The bright stable lights reflected off the inside of the window glass, making us invisible as we stood outside watching.

We waited, shivering in the cold, for what seemed like a long time, and then Donny finally appeared. He was dressed in what he had now come to think of as *his* police uniform. As we watched, he looked around nervously a couple of times and then entered one of the stalls.

Warren and I were by now seasoned policemen and had seen a lot over the years, but what we witnessed in the stall that night nearly floored us. What made it worse was that Donny's unnatural attentions were directed at Warren's horse and he was a gelding.

"For Christ's sake!" Warren was leaning back on the fire escape railing, breathing like he had just finished the hundred-yard dash and mumbling to himself, "the dirty, dirty bastard!"

Then he turned on me. "This was all your idea, you smart ass. So what do we do now? We could lose our jobs. If we arrest him, he'll blab the whole thing, Christ, how will it look in the papers?"

I thought a little humour would calm him down, so I tried, "C'mon, Warren, he was doing a great job until this small infraction."

He wasn't amused and I thought he was going to kill me.

"Okay, okay!" I said, "I'll take care of it."

"Yeah? What are you going to do?" he snarled.

"Don't worry, I'm not going to arrest him. How would that look: sexual assault on a police horse?"

We made a lot of noise outside the stable to announce our arrival, and when we entered Donny emerged from the stalls looking nervous and uncomfortable, though not as nervous and uncomfortable as Warren. He had to book off for the rest of the shift, sick to his stomach.

I took Donny into the lunchroom, sat him down on a chair at the opposite side of the table and confronted him with what he had done. I had talked with Donny a bit over the months and I knew he was under the care of a psychiatrist, though I didn't know he was seeing him because of an unnatural attraction to horses and other barnyard animals. I got the doctor's name and number before I sent Donny on his way, asking him never to return.

The next day I contacted his doctor, and he assured me that he would see Donny right away and deal with the matter, then thanked me for my understanding. I thought the matter was over, and after a couple of months Warren even started talking to me again and we put the whole thing behind us.

About a year later, Donny was taken into custody on an unrelated matter and he blabbed the whole story. The investigating detectives thought he was nuts: nothing that unbelievable could ever have happened.

40: Working with Merle

Merle Smith had recently lost his breaking and training partner. Bert Boardman had resigned so that he could devote all his time to an office cleaning business he had been moonlighting at for a couple of years. Strange choice for a former member of the Queen's Household Cavalry and longtime mounted man...but go figure.

I was worried that Merle might resent the fact that a young whipper-snapper like me was going to be Bert's replacement, but as things turned out my fears were unfounded and he welcomed me, and we got along really well.

He was a tall, athletically-built man in his early forties, dark black hair receding over his temples, healthy-looking but always pale from the end-less hours he spent inside the Horse Palace. Most importantly to me, he was a good man with the horses. When he put his big hands on them, they knew he meant business, but he was always kind and fair with them, rewarding them when they performed well and gently punishing them when they did not.

He didn't talk a great deal about his personal life with me or any of the other guys; it was all horse talk. His main passion other than the horses was playing Bump with the other officers on his lunch hour. He sure loved those dominoes.

We trained several horses while we worked together, but the pair I re-member the most were two western horses that the Department bought from Alex Stewart. Merle worked on a big chestnut half-thoroughbred named Sandy and I had a black gelding about the same size aptly named Blackie. Both of these horses had spent most of their lives running free on the Alberta prairies and were not easy to break.

At one point, when we had been repeatedly deposited on our asses on the tanbark, we seriously considered returning them to that old fox, Alex. However, I had recently bought some horses, for my own use from the old horse trader and was looking for more; he convinced me that if I would persevere with Blackie and convince Merle to do the same with Sandy I might be looking at some pretty good deals down the road.

It wasn't that difficult getting Merle to stay at it with Sandy; he seemed to have real affection for the animal. Even much later on, when we finally got both animals quiet to ride and Sandy developed Sit Fasts on his back and had to undergo major surgery to remove them, Merle nursed him constantly, coming in on his days off to make sure he was alright.

As it turned out, Blackie and Sandy both turned out to be excellent police horses. I noticed that Merle spent a lot more time than he usually did explaining how she should be treated when he handed her over to the cop who would use her on the streets.

Merle and I only had one major disagreement during the time we worked together. It was over a horse named Monty, a big, ugly bay gelding that someone had talked the Inspector into buying. The horse was about six years old and had had some training, but he came our way because the lady who had owned him couldn't handle him anymore and, I suppose, because the price was right.

Merle had a go at him at first, but soon became disgusted with his antics. He was stubborn as a mule and absolutely refused to respond to Merle's attempts to teach him to neck rein. When he felt he had spent enough time in the riding ring, he would simply head for the door and no amount of whoahing or hauling on the reins would dissuade him.

He also, for no particular reason, occasionally stood on his hind legs and pawed the air with his front ones. As dramatic a picture this paints, it was very unsettling, because whoever was riding him was in danger of sliding off the saddle and over his rump on the way to the ground. It was after dismounting in this fashion for the third time that Merle decided that the horse was a lost cause.

I'm sure that Merle, had he stayed with it, would have mastered the animal, but, as he calmly put it when he finally handed me the reins, "We don't get along!"

I was pretty sure I had a remedy for the big bay's nonsense, but I wasn't sure what Merle's reaction would be when I told him what I was going to do. I had had quite a bit of experience working with difficult horses in the past, but I deliberately played my cards close to my chest. I didn't want to appear like a smart-ass know-it all, and up until now I had always asked his advice, even though the questions were for the most part rhetorical.

The next day I brought in an antique copy of Magner's *Horse and Stock*

Book. I pretended that I had just discovered the book and was anxious to

try some of the horse-breaking techniques it described. In reality I had owned the book and many more like it for years and had tried and proved most of the tricks they suggested.

Still I kept up the charade, slipped the book in front of Merle and opened it at a page I had marked. The topic I showed him was called "Subjection" and what it described was a good, humane way to throw a horse, or, more accurately, ease him to the ground. The theory was that a difficult horse subjected to this treatment would feel totally dominated and instantly develop a new and improved attitude.

Merle was not shy about telling me that he thought it was a bad idea and that it probably wouldn't work. "Go ahead if you want to, but I'm not going to have anything to do with it," he said. "If you get in trouble, you're on your own, buddy!"

I knew it would work, and it did.

To my surprise Merle was never jealous or pissy about what happened, and over the following months I used the technique whenever Monty took a bad spell and needed a tune-up. I think his original reticence was because he was worried that I might injure the horse; Merle was the kind of guy who wouldn't harm a fly unnecessarily.

That's why I was so surprised and shocked, a year after I left the job, to hear that he had shot and killed his estranged wife and her lover.

In a crime of passion, there usually is a hell of a lot more to the story than meets the eye, and in this case I know there was. I prefer to remember him as the quiet man who loved horses.

Garry Leeson

41: Windy Hill

Policemen were not allowed to live outside the limits of Metropolitan Toronto. Before the amalgamation in 1998 they were restricted to the limits of the old city of Toronto proper.

I suppose in the old days this policy had some merit. Few people had cars and transportation in general was quite slow, so the city wanted their policemen close at hand and ready to respond in emergencies. This arrangement also made it convenient for the Department to control malingering, because anytime a cop phoned in sick he would get a mandatory visit from patrol sergeant and the patient had better be in bed with a temperature and no booze on his breath when he got there, or he was in deep shit.

We were allowed sick days but, other than when I was badly injured or actually in the hospital, I don't remember daring to call in sick.

I longed to live in the country. My parents had a farm near Meaford, Ontario and I spent all my spare time up there. I had several horses and some purebred Angus cattle that I kept there, but it was too far away for a commute, and even if I could have the Department would never have allowed it.

I was always on the lookout for a rental farm closer to the city, and recent events gave my search a certain urgency, I knew it was probably wishful thinking, but it was fun cruising the countryside, dreaming of finding that special place.

Here's what happened: for some reason that I never fully understood, a representative from Ayerst Laboratories of Montreal contacted me and asked if I would meet with him. Of course I was curious and agreed to see him, even though I didn't have the slightest notion of what he wanted.

As it turned out he wanted to offer me quite a good job. They were the people who produced the newly-arrived birth control pill and they wanted me to head up a team of special inspectors.

In those days all of the estrogen used in the production of the pill

166

came naturally from the urine of pregnant mares. Special stables were springing up all over the country to meet the demand and the company was under pressure from The Humane Society and other groups to ensure that proper practices were observed.

I was having too much fun doing what I was doing so I immediately declined his offer but said I would ask around and see if anybody else I knew would be interested.

As it turned out, when I mentioned it at the stables the following week, half the guys on the unit expressed interest. Sergeant Quinn, the riding instructor, was most eager, and in a matter of days was flown up to Montreal and given the job.

Later it looked like I had connived the whole thing because I ended up getting his job teaching new recruits; it was, however, pure coincidence.

He later recruited two more people from the unit. The Inspector was sad to see them go but, in true form, wished them all the best. I kept my head down for a while.

I wasn't interested in the job with Ayerst, but after I researched the methods used to collect the urine I was sure I could improve on them and was anxious to give it a try with my own place and band of mares. Besides, there was big money in the business. I knew I would be a shoo-in because Sergeant Quinn was now in charge of issuing the contracts.

If I was careful, really careful, no one would find out and I would be able to keep my job.

One day I strayed to the area around Chalk Lake, north of Oshawa, and happened on a small, neat farmstead perched on the top of a hill that thrust itself out of a large cedar grove. I followed the lane up through the trees to the buildings, and from there I could see acres of well-groomed fields, fenced with split rails, stretching off into the distance. A herd of Shorthorn cattle currently occupied the pasture, but I mentally replaced them with horses and sure liked what I saw.

I don't know what had given me the audacity to barge, uninvited, unto this hilltop homestead. There were no for sale or for rent signs, I had arrived where I stood purely on the wings of impulse.

No one appeared to be home, but I thought I had better check for sure, so I went to the house ready to apologize for my intrusion.

There was no answer to my knock, so I ventured a peek through the window. The house was empty and appeared to have been that way for some time. There were no electric lines leading up to the house and, as I circled the place peering through the windows, I could tell that there never had been any wiring in the house.

What the hell, no one was around, so I decided to check out the barn as well. It had been left clean and tidy and the cement and steel stanchions suggested that it had once housed a large herd of milk cows. It would take quite a bit of work, but they could be converted into horse stalls.

I walked through the pasture all the way to the next concession line, to where I knew the property must end, and estimated it to be about one hundred acres. Perfect!

It was fun to pretend that places such as this were yours, and I had dreamed these dreams before, but something about this spot compelled me to find out more, so I decided to drop in on the next-door neighbour and have a chat.

The next farm was occupied by an aging widow and her two rather strange bachelor sons.

Buster, the weirder of the two, was a wealth of information. He told me that the old farm I had been investigating had been sold recently to a young couple who lived in a village nearby. They had no immediate plans for the place and might consider renting it out. He and his brother were already renting a couple of the fields to grow grain.

I found the owners on the way home and started discussions that eventually saw me signing a three-year lease.

Things were becoming very complicated for me. On the one hand I needed the place to accommodate my project but, on the other, I would be jeopardizing a job that I had come to love. I needed a plan.

I couldn't afford to keep my apartment in the city and pay rent on the farm, but I still needed an address that appeared to be legitimate within the confines of the city. I had previously rented a small room on the second floor of my friend Ron Bond's house, down by The Beaches area of the city, and he was more than willing to start collecting rent again. It was a good deal since I actually wouldn't be there. I thought I could trust him to keep our little secret.

I moved to the farm, brought my Angus cattle down from my parents' farm, purchased an Arabian stallion and started buying brood mares. Everything was going as planned and, best of all, it was all happening under Big Ed's nose.

I sure had the big guy fooled, at least that is what I thought until one day he called me into his office and made a request. "I've got two lame horses and Monty is acting up again; I think a few weeks on pasture would do them all good," he said looking me in the eye then pausing waiting for me to reply.

"Yes, no doubt it would, sir." I was well aware of the horses' conditions.

"You wouldn't know a place in the country, not too far away, where I could pasture them, would you?"

I could tell by the look on his face that the jig was up; he was just toy-ing with me. All the work I had put into the farm's house and barn and all the money I had spent buying horses was about to go up in smoke.

He broke into a smile and said, "Relax. I knew about your farm before you moved in. I don't blame you for wanting to live there; as far as I'm concerned your address in the city covers you. I don't know what headquarters will think about it, but we'll cross that bridge when we come to it. In the meantime, I'm serious about needing pasture for those horses, so what are you going to charge me?"

"Let's consider it a professional courtesy," I replied.

Over the next year or so the police horse trailer spent as much time parked at 'Windy Hill', the name I had given my place, as it did down in the city.

42: The Hamilton paddy wagon

One day, when I went to check on some police horses in the Horse Palace, I found a strange horse standing in one of the stalls. It was a little bay quarter horse, about half the size of the other horses. The gelding stood with its head down, looking tired and dejected, switching his weight from one lame front foot to the other.

I had noticed the Inspector's car parked outside, and now, as my eyes adjusted to the dim light of the stable, I saw him down the aisle, in conversation with three large policemen in traditional turn-of-the-century uniforms, complete with bobby helmets.

They seemed to be looking at something around the corner, and when I went over to join them I was surprised to see the object of their attention, an authentic antique, horse-drawn paddy wagon, complete in every detail and fully restored.

The men could see that I was curious and weren't long filling me in with what was going on. The Hamilton Police Department, as part of a Centennial project, had refurbished the old wagon and the men present were part of a team that had been chosen to drive it all the way to Montreal for the opening of Expo 67.

The idea, as it turned out, was a sound one, but the horse was not. It was neither big enough nor strong enough to pull a wagon of that size and they had been damned lucky to get the fifty miles from Hamilton to Toronto, let alone the three hundred and fifty still to go before they reached their destination.

When I interrupted them, they were busy trying to borrow one of the Toronto police horses for the job and Big Ed was trying to explain to them that our horses were not broken to harness and that, even if they were, Expo would probably be over by the time he swam through the red tape it would take to get permission to use one of them.

I felt sorry for the guys from Hamilton and wanted to help. I could see that they were really disappointed and embarrassed that their project was about to come to such an abrupt end.

As it happened, I had purchased a couple of really big Percheron mares for my estrogen project. One of them, a big docile bay, was quiet enough that even these rank amateurs would be able to handle her, so I offered to let them use her. She was in foal, but I was sure that a little road trip wouldn't hurt her.

I heard from the men later that she performed wonderfully, and after the first few miles they just let her have her head and she strode along the shoulder of the highway, undeterred by the speeding trucks and cars, getting them to Montreal in plenty of time.

After she returned home in style in a fancy racehorse van, the inspector found a small, old Toronto police wagon, and Ron Bond and I drove her in several parades during the Centennial celebrations.

1967 was a hell of a year for me. I divided my time between the excitement of police work, parades and musical rides, and the busy weekends breeding mares, preparing for my new business and enjoying my new country lifestyle.

Then everything started to go wrong. A scientist somewhere discovered how to synthesize estrogen, and mare's urine was no longer required,

I practically begged my former Sergeant, Bob Quinn, to get Ayerst to honour the contract we had signed, but he drew my attention to the fine print, and I knew I was screwed. I couldn't get mad at him, because I knew that his job was also in jeopardy. He said that the company had offered him an office job, but I knew that the old cowboy from Little Buckhorn wouldn't be long riding a desk.

I was stuck with thirty or so horses, most in foal, with no way to make any economic sense out of them. A dark cloud was hanging over Windy Hill.

43: And then there was this

Just when you think that things can't get any worse, they usually do. That's what I was thinking when I was summoned into Inspector Johnson's office on a Friday afternoon.

"I've had a call from headquarters concerning you," he said

Great! I thought, *Just what I need. They've found out about the farm and I'm in deep shit!*

But apparently that was not what this was all about because the Inspector just passed a file folder across his desk to me, saying, "What's this all about?"

The brown manila file folder was stamped with the familiar logo of the Toronto Parks Department. I had no idea what it might contain.

When I opened it, I felt like I had bumped into an old friend. Inside was a proposal that I had drafted and submitted to the Parks Deptartment when I was seventeen years old. I had forgotten all about it and now, as I flicked through the typed pages and illustrations I had done, I wondered why it had surfaced after all these years. The reply I had received at the time was curt and condescending and I was surprised that they kept the idea on their records.

When I was a teenager attending high school, I had a small stable on Bayview Avenue, on a ridge above the Don River Valley. I made a little extra money giving riding lessons and taking people on trail rides, south along the river through the old Sunnybrook Farm. At the time the Parks Department did not have responsibility for the area, but it was rumored that they might in the future.

I was fascinated with the beautiful structures that stood unused; it uas like a ghost village hidden in the heart of the city. The barns in particular took my eye, and I reasoned that if in fact the area was to become a public park, it would be a wonderful opportunity to establish a riding school and designate bridle paths.

As I read more carefully through the pages of recommendations that I had made almost seven years earlier I wondered at how naive and full of lofty ideals I must have been to even think that a kid from Cabbage Town would be listened to.

Under the photocopies of my old submission I found a copy of a tender application for obtaining a concession to operate a riding school at the old Sunnybrook Farm. It was to be the focal point of the newly-established Central Don Park System. The descriptions of how it was to operate and what needed to be done to the existing buildings were taken verbatim from my original submission.

Inspector Johnson had been called to a meeting the day previous with Tommy Thompson, who was the current flamboyant parks commissioner, to discuss the possibility of the mounted unit moving their headquarters to the newly-established park, an idea Big Ed was instantly in favour of, when the issue of a public riding school sharing the accommodation came up. He was asked his opinion and then passed the file, and while reading through it, he happened to see my submission. He immediately recognized my name and explained to the commissioner that I was currently serving in his unit.

This came as surprise to the clerk in charge of the tender process. Apparently they had been trying to locate me to invite me to tender, but so much time had passed and I had changed addresses so often that they had been unable to locate me.

I think the Inspector and the people from the Park's Department realized that with one of their own, as it were, in charge of the public riding school, the relationship between it and the Police Department was bound to better than if some stranger were to move in next door. Apparently it was Inspector Johnson's assignment to talk me into submitting a tender and, quite frankly he was doing a hell of a job. He assured me that I had nothing to lose and everything to gain. If things didn't work out, I could always have my job on the mounted unit back.

I mulled it over, but not for long. I submitted my tender like everyone else, offering twelve hundred dollars a month for the facilities, a huge sum for me in those days. In retrospect, I could have offered a lot less because other considerations were in play and the process was less a competition and more in the order of an appointment.

Anyhow, my tender was accepted and a new chapter in my life began.

I had just been given a wonderful opportunity to do something that had been on my mind for years. I wanted to establish a riding school that would be affordable and available to anybody who wanted to use it. I had grown up for the most part an inner-city kid; I loved horses but had very little opportunity to spend much time with them. I knew every delivery horse in the city, but my riding experience, when I was very young, was limited to a few hours a month.

I would ride the old Young Street trolley to the city limits at Hog's Hollow and then hike the rest of the way to Vern Mason's riding school. It used to be situated further up in the Don Valley. If I spent the morning mucking out stalls for him, I was allowed to go out on a one-hour trail ride. Later, as he realized that I had a certain natural ability, he would occasionally use me to lead these rides.

There were kids like me all over the city, and there still were now. I had seen their interest as I rode the police horses around the city. I knew that there were thousands of people, young and old, who would love the opportunity to be near to and learn about horses.

In my early teens I had eventually made my way out of the city and had the opportunity to improve my skills, spending long hours in the saddle, breaking and training young horses. Eventually I felt that there was very little that I couldn't do with a horse.

However, I got my training at The School of Hard Knocks, the only academy I could afford, and it irked me to think that learning to ride was still only available to the privileged few who could afford to pay for the fancy gear and the expensive lessons.

I had a wonderful new stable of my own design now, and I also had a mission.

PONY RIDES

The Central Don hasn't forgotten the tiny tot. A number of small ponies are available to be used for short rides for children not yet ready for lessons or trail rides.

These ponies are rented by the half hour. They are led by the parent or any responsible adult that brings the child. This creates an opportunity for an outing where both the parent and child can participate.

TRAIL RIDES

Quiet trail rides through miles of beautiful parkland are available on weekends and week day evenings (all day every day during summer vacation). These rides are designed for the casual rider. It is hoped that these rides will encourage the novice rider to take part in riding classes and improve his skill.

HAY RIDES

Old fashioned hay rides are available for group outings. This activity can be used to highlight a weiner roast or cookout at any of the many public campsites throughout the park.

So if it's a youth group, social club, class party or just a friendly outing in the park be sure to take advantage of this interesting and unusual activity.

SLEIGH RIDES

During the winter months the traditional, bright coloured sleighs are used in place of the summer hay wagons and with the addition of some sleigh bells and beautiful winter scenery it adds up to an experience to be remembered.

Tobaggans and warm refreshments supplied at no extra cost.

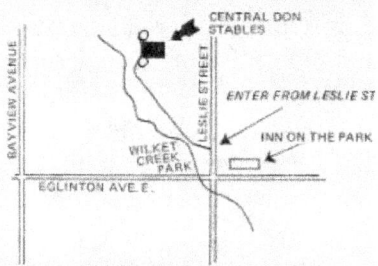

SO NEAR YET SO VERY FAR AWAY
IN THE HEART OF METRO

CENTRAL DON STABLES

445 - 7337

44: No place for a horse

My wife, Andrea, and I were on vacation walking through a small Scottish village a few years ago when I noticed a strange nasty, overpowering odor in the air—burning coal! I knew that smell. It was a blast from the past.

Certain smells trigger memories. It's called "the Proust effect"—that whiff of the smoke was sending me on a nostalgic journey back to my early childhood in Toronto.

Until the 1960s, the city still depended on coal for domestic heating, electricity generation, consumer gas production and its numerous steam-powered train engines. With its dark, stained skyscrapers and polluted air it was the quintessential "Dirty Old Town" of Canada. There was always the pervasive smell of burning coal in the air in those days, but it was not a singular scent.

Most people (but not me!) complained that there was another, equally obnoxious, odour contributing to the urban pong. Personally, I have never found the warm, spicy aroma of horse manure all that offensive.

Preferences aside, there was no getting away from the fact that the whole city, summer and winter, was always enveloped in a pungent bouquet of those two very different fragrances.

In 1945, when I moved with my family to Toronto, there were few motor vehicles in the city but still thousands of horses working in the streets. My aunt's house, where we first stayed, was just around the corner from Borden's Dairy, the largest in the city. Early each morning in front of the house there would be a long line of over fifty horses and their milk wagons waiting their turn to move along to the dairy's main building, where they would fill up with milk, butter and cream to deliver.

All over the city, while most people slept, a similar scene was playing out at dairies, bakeries and department store warehouses, with hundreds of delivery wagons stocking up for their early morning deliveries. Almost anything that needed to be transported in the big city did so with the aid of horses.

Later in the day the coal wagons, pulled by a three-horse hitch of heavy draft horses, would supply the population with their main source of heat and, similarly, ice wagons would provide the city's only option for domestic refrigeration.

There was still a scattering of fruit vendors, with placid nags wearing straw hats, plying the streets, as well as junk collectors in rickety rigs patrolling the back alleys.

But for the advent of World War Two, a total transition from horsepower to motorized vehicles might have been accomplished much earlier. In fact, the changeover had already begun in earnest before the war started, and was well on its way when gas rationing and the production of motor vehicles ceased.

At that point, all the companies that could, parked their motorized trucks and vans, purchased fresh horses and new harness, and reacquired and refurbished the delivery wagons they had so recently sold off. Once again the streets were filled with horses and wagons.

The war ended and the attrition of the city's equine fleet began again. What had been instigated as a patriotic endeavour on the part of the companies was short-lived. One by one, the quiet, faithful animals that had been so commonplace as they worked their routes through the residential areas of the city began to disappear until, finally, there was no longer any reason for kids like me to carry carrots and sugar cubes in their pockets.

I grew up thinking of those times fondly. I guess that's why I was comfortable joining the police force, and riding and training some of the last horses that would ever be a familiar sight in the city.

In 1963, when I joined, there were still seven active police stables distributed throughout the city, housing around sixty horses. The hundreds of other buildings that once supported the equine infrastructure were preserved, but most had been converted to different uses. Most notably, the iconic Coxwell Stables, that once housed the city's large complement of horses used in the collection of garbage and clean street maintenance, was converted to affordable housing units.

In 1967, when I assisted a fellow constable to rescue and seize a lame rag and bone collector's horse, I presumed that the days of the city horse, other than police mounts, had finally come to an end. I couldn't have predicted that, a year later, I would be the owner and operator of a new, large stable in the heart of the city.

I had always had the naive notion that it would be good if, somehow, we could turn back the clock and relive the good old days when the horse reigned supreme in the city. But the reality of the situation was very different.

My business, Central Don Stables, was located in a hidden valley in a large park complex and it mimicked a safe, pastoral environment. In the confines of the park, the horses might have been on a farm somewhere, but ride or drive just a few yards out of its boundaries and you would find yourself in a whirlwind of speeding cars and trucks driven by people who knew nothing and cared less about the safety of you or your horses.

Because I had quiet horses that were used to traffic, I occasionally braved the busy city streets to do various promotions. I was lucky enough to be spared anything like the horrific accidents involving carriage horses that were being reported in other cities—but it had become a dangerous game that I tried to avoid.

When I sold my business in 1972 and my wife and I moved away from the city to a farm in Nova Scotia, I was still clinging to the notion that, in some circumstances, there might still be a place in an urban environment for horses. I was remembering a time when horses were able to move safely through shaded streets devoid of automobiles and most were housed in well-kept, often heated, multi level stables. A time when the quality and condition of the animals reflected on the company that owned them and there was a constant competition to own, maintain and display them at their best.

All of these fond memories were dashed for me a few years ago while strolling through Times Square in New York City.

I noticed a handsome dapple-grey gelding hitched to a fancy carriage, waiting by the curb. Traffic had stopped momentarily and couldn't resist the urge to get up closer.

I was smiling up at the carriage driver and stroking the gelding's neck when the lights changed and a long line of yellow cabs started buzzing by. As each cab approached, then passed, I felt the horse begin to tremble under my hand, and when I stepped forward to check behind his blinkers I could see that each time a cab approached, his eyes would squint into a terrified grimace.

In all the years I had spent around them I had never seen a horse react or show fear like that. All my illusions about the possibility of still safely using horses in a city were instantly swept away. That frightened horse was telling me how wrong I had been.

The city of today is "No Place for a Horse."

45: Saving Peggy

It was unusual to see old police horses on the streets of Toronto. The policy was to foster them out to good homes while they still had some useful years ahead of them. There was always a long list of people anxious to adopt them; they were so quiet, safe and dependable it was almost like acquiring an insurance policy.

The people making the decision when to farm them out were faced with a dilemma; the animals didn't have Best Before labels, they were a valuable commodity and the trick was to get the maximum number of years out of them and still leave them with enough health and vitality to make them attractive to the people who might provide them with quiet country homes in their dotage.

It wasn't always just a practical issue. Often officers and horses had been paired up for years and had formed strong emotional attachments. It wasn't unusual for those in charge to put off placing a horse for a couple of years so that it would coincide with the retirement of the cop who rode him. I guess it was because of this that you occasionally saw an officer with grey around his temples riding a horse with grey over the eyes.

It's been a long time, but whenever I'm able to conjure up a vision of somebody I served with I always see his horse standing beside him. Pat Wolfe with Duchess, Ron Bond with Joe, Merle Smith with Sandy, and on and on.

Sometimes a horse would face early retirement because they received a permanent injury or become sore-footed from the constant pounding on the pavement. Roy Cardy had to part with his mount Peggy prematurely because she injured her fetlock and was no longer up to the heavy work required of her. She was a real old treasure, a very dark bay, comical to look at with her oversized head and one slightly lopped off ear. It was a sad day for Roy when he had to part with her, but he consoled himself with the knowledge that she was going to a good home.

While they were with the mounted unit, the horses lived a good life, well fed and looked after, almost pampered. Even after I left the job I kept an eye out for suitable remounts for the Department; I had already found a couple and I knew they were going to a good home. Inspector Johnson seemed to value my judgment and purchased them without question.

I was buying and selling a lot of horses at the time and attended all the auctions and regularly made my rounds of the horse dealers: Alec Picou in Oshawa, Alex Stewart at the Toronto Stock Yards, Less Erhlick in the heart of the city, Vern Mason in Richmond hill and Albert Greco in Kleinberg; plus, all the special auctions and the regular weekly one at Kitchener Livestock Sales.

Alec Stewart gave me a call to say he had a couple of "second-hand horses", as he called them, to show me. These were usually older horses that his clients had traded in on the fancy, pure-bred stock that he imported. He knew that I was more interested in quiet temperaments than I was in breeding and good looks. Some of the most useful school horses that I used at my stable had come out of his pens.

Alec kept his horses at the old stockyards in the northwest corner of the city, using a few of the pens you first encountered as you entered through the main gates. The entire facility was about twenty acres of neat, orderly, whitewashed pens separated by narrow cobbled alleyways, all covered by one low roof that kept the place in a constant state of semi darkness. The horse stalls that Alec kept benefited from the light from a bank of windows along an outside wall, but if you ventured further in you were enveloped in the gloom of the place and bombarded by the cries of thousands of doomed cattle, sheep and pigs waiting their turn to enter the big centre aisle, where they would follow the Judas steer to the slaughterhouses on the north side of Keele Street.

A certain class of horses termed meat horses were not exempt from a similar fate. I knew where the pens were that held those poor creatures, but I tried not to think about them and seldom went there.

When I arrived at the yards early one morning I first checked the restaurant in the basement of the main building for Alex. He had already finished his habitual bacon and eggs and headed out to see to his horses.

When I found him, he was standing on a bale of hay, peering over the fence into one of his pens. I liked the old guy. He was the last of his breed; an agile seventy-two years of age at the time, still tall and erect and bright as a penny. He was always dressed to the nines no matter where he was or what he was doing, with jacket and tie and highly polished shoes topped, when he was in the stable, with a long raincoat with a bamboo cane hanging from an inside pocket.

When he saw me, he tilted back his grey fedora and beckoned me over. "See that sorrel mare in the corner?" he asked "How tall would you say she was?"

I climbed up the rails to have a better look. "Oh, I dunno maybe about 15. 2."

"That's what I was thinking," he said. "But I've got to be sure because I've got some people coming to buy her. Listen, you're younger than me. Climb in there and measure her for me."

"Okee Dokee," I said as I swung over the top rail and dropped into the pen. He unhooked the cane from inside his slicker and handed it to me through the rails of the fence.

I loved that cane. Hidden inside the shaft was a long, narrow, telescopic ruler with a flip-out arm with a level on the top.

I backed the mare into a corner, and she stood quietly while I held the cane ruler against her shoulder, extracted the ruler and settled the level arm down on her withers.

"I guess we were both wrong," I said when I got back to Alex. "She's about 15.3. She'll be sixteen hands with shoes on."

"All the better," he beamed.

Then I surrendered his wonderful antique cane to him, jokingly restating my desire that he leave it to me in his will.

By now, his customers had found their way to his area of the yards and, as they approached where we were standing, he pointed down the alleyway in the opposite direction. "Go down to pen number 23. That's where those horses I told you about are."

I can take a hint, so I made myself scarce and headed in the direction he indicated. He didn't like me around when he priced his horses to the general public, because he knew that I knew that they were generally worth about half as much as he was asking.

Anyway, I busied myself in the wholesale division of his establishment, picking out a couple of geldings, an old Palomino and a little bay Standard Bred with a star on his forehead. I tried each of them out, riding them around the pen bareback and steering them with the top strap of their halter. They seemed to know what they were doing; if the price was right they would be coming home with me.

Alec was still busy with his customers when I finished trying out the horses I was interested in, so I wandered off into the inner part of the yards to kill time.

I was thinking about something else as I wandered through the aisles and was surprised when I found myself next to the pens that contained the meat horses. My first instinct was to turn and walk the other way, but some weird compulsion drew me to the pens where I climbed the rails for a closer look.

The scene was as I expected; about a dozen dejected-looking horses, mostly heavy draft animals in poor condition with heavy winter coats. They had obviously been kept outside all winter. There was very little colour variation in the group, all blacks or dark bays with occasional white patches on their backs and shoulders where they had been galled by years of work in harness. Most stood with their heads hanging puffing wisps of frozen vapour that rose and hung over the pen in a low, thin static cloud. Some stood on three legs, nursing old injuries, while others hunkered back on their hind quarters to relieve the pressure on their foundered front feet.

It was a sad lot, but there was nothing I could do about it. I figured the sooner they got put out of their misery the better.

But one animal caught my eye. She seemed more animated than the rest, moving around the pen, weaving in and out of the other animals and going over to the long manger periodically to grab mouthfuls of hay. She didn't show as much draft blood as the rest of the group; her hair was incredibly long, and it made her body seem thicker and fuller than it really was.

As I climbed down to leave she came forward and hung her head over the top rail directly in front of me.

That's when I noticed it; it hadn't been noticeable at a distance because her hair was so long, even the fuzz on her ears, but now I could see it: her right ear was not pointed like the left. It was shorter, with a blunt straight top.

I couldn't believe my eyes, but as I imagined her with a short and shiny coat, without the long hair and the pellets of dung that adhered to her rear end, I knew it must be her.

I climbed back up and over the rail, grabbed hold of her halter and eased myself on to her back. I pulled back gently and whispered, "Back, back."

She responded immediately. When we were in the middle of the pen I moved her around, neck-reining her in both directions. She turned without hesitation.

Then I gave her the final test. Halting her and restricting her forward motion I applied my right leg to her flank. She did a perfect side passage to the left sweeping the other horses out of her way as she went.

"Well, for Christ's sake, it is you, Peggy, old girl!" I said as I slid down off her back rubbing her eyes and making much of her.

The swelling on her fetlock confirmed the obvious, so I told her to wait while I went to see if I could spring her.

The agent in charge was reluctant to do business with me because he said the whole group of horses had been spoken for. He changed his mind when I offered him double the going price of fifteen cents a pound, and we weren't long weighing her and him pocketing the three hundred and thirty dollars cash I gave him.

As I led her over to Alec's stalls, I was pleased to see that she wasn't limping or favouring her old injury. I put her in the pen with my other purchases, and before the day was out they were all trucked to the safety of my stables.

I couldn't wait to tell Big Ed about rescuing Peggy, but I wanted to clean her up a bit first, so I waited till the next morning. Overnight I decided that I would have a little fun with him, so devised a plan.

He lived in the cottage next to mine at Sunnybrook, and I made sure I was waiting at the paddock fence as he made his way over to his office the next morning. I had already turned Peggy loose in the enclosure and placed some hay in a corner furthest from where I stood waiting for the inspector to pass.

He grunted "Good morning," and I started right in on him.

"Look over there, Inspector. I've got another new horse for you."

He squinted in her direction for a while then said, "Well, she looks the right sort from here, a little rough but she'd probably clean up. How old is she?"

"Ya know, I'm not quite sure. Why don't you come over with me and we'll check her mouth."

The horse stood still and watched us as we opened the gate and headed over to her. I grabbed the fancy new halter I had put on her while the Inspector parted her lips and looked in her mouth.

He looked a little startled when he saw the length of her teeth; then something dawned on him and, without a word, he reached up and caressed her chopped-off ear then, still remaining silent, knelt down and felt for her injured fetlock.

He uttered one word and I started explaining.

As my story unfolded, his face became redder and redder until I thought the top of his head was about to blow off. When I finished he turned and marched purposefully toward his office, I knew he was a man on a mission, and I pitied the person who had betrayed his trust and sold

Peggy down the river.

I never found out exactly how he handled the matter, but I made darn sure that the home I subsequently found for her was the very best, and I know she enjoyed her remaining years until, much later, she was finally laid to rest in an orchard next to her pasture.

46: Show Biz

One Friday afternoon I found myself sharing a few pints with Ron Bond and some other friends at a downtown Toronto watering hole called the Coal Bin. We went there frequently, especially at the end of the week, and we liked to arrive fairly early so we would be ready when the offices in the huge highrises, directly across the road, closed down and all the secretaries hit the bar for a quick "Thank God it's Friday" cocktail.

We knew that, as good as their intentions might be, when the band started playing their resolve would fly out the window and hurrying home would be forgotten. It was almost impossible to get out of that place alone when the lights began flashing at closing time.

It was the era of free love, and it was almost as if gratuitous sex had replaced the handshake as a form of greeting.

On this particular Friday we made an unusually early start, getting to the bar for lunch. Ron wanted to have a little extra time to build up some liquid courage before the lovelies started arriving. He hadn't been having much luck lately and was determined, as he put it, to cut a weak one out of the herd that evening.

For my part, I was feeling down in the dumps. I think I was getting tired of the whole sordid lifestyle. It was just one meaningless encounter after the other. Don't get me wrong: they were all wonderful women, but there were so many of them and so little time. There had to be something else.

When the bar started to fill up and the band arrived, Ron and my other friends started getting up periodically to chat up some girl and thrash around on the dance floor. I wasn't in the mood so I kept to myself and just sat, frequently refilling my mug from the large pitchers of draft that kept appearing on the table.

I guess my mood was infectious because, as the afternoon wore on, the boys were spending less and less time on the dance floor and more and more time seated around the huge barrel that served as our table.

We had all gone to the same technical high school together and one of the guys mentioned that he thought it strange that none of us was actually working in the field we had trained for. He made it sound as if we were all failures for not becoming the draftsmen and machinists we had planned to be.

I had tried to work as mechanical draftsman for a while, but the only job I could find was drawing sewers for the city and I figured that that was about as low as I could go, so I quit and finally ended up on the police force before starting a business of my own.

The guys pointed out that my riding school was no small achievement, but I was not to be consoled, I knew something was missing in my life, and the more I drank, the larger the void became.

The other guys started talking about their current occupations and what they would rather be doing, and it was truly surprising to listen to their previously-undisclosed aspirations.

Ron Bond claimed he wanted to become an author. When I brought it to his attention that I had never seen him with a book in his hand he got all huffy and slurred, "I don't read books, I write books!"

Braving the ridicule, one by one, the rest of the guys divulged their secret hopes. When it became my turn to share, for no apparent reason, I heard myself saying, "I have always wanted to be an actor!"

I just blurted it out. For the life of me, I don't know where it came from. It wasn't even close to being true. Maybe a playbill that had been left lying on the table by a previous customer was influencing me subliminally, or maybe it was pure one-upmanship. Whatever the reason, I did say it and now was compelled to stick to my story.

Of course, my old friend Ron led the attack on me saying, "I've known you for years and you've never mentioned anything like this before. You must be drunk or crazy."

I hit him with my favourite W.C. Fields quote: "I may be drunk but you're the one who is crazy. Tomorrow I'll be sober and you'll still be crazy!"

The other guys laughed but Ron had heard me use that line too often in the past and continued his interrogation undeterred.

He could be pretty relentless when criticizing me, and for the next twenty minutes or so he pulled out all the stops, drawing all my shortcomings to my attention. He was getting my Irish dander up and I was just about to offer him a knuckle sandwich when he delivered a final salvo that stopped me in my tracks. "If you were really serious about this you'd go and apply for a job as an actor—now!"

"Maybe I will, you asshole!" I shot back at him, turning away dismissively and hoping that would be the end of the discussion.

No such luck. One of the other guys, trying to be helpful, mentioned that the CBC casting office was just around the corner and that maybe that would be a good place for me to start my career.

This was just the fresh ammunition that Ron needed, and he renewed his attack, daring me to put my money where my mouth was. I countered with an offer to go up to the casting office as soon as he finished the first chapter of the book he was planning to write, but he wasn't to be put off and I found myself swearing in front of all present that I would go for an interview that very afternoon.

The boys were not a trusting lot, and shortly afterwards they escorted me around the corner and watched while I entered the main foyer of the CBC building. They were still watching me through the glass doors as I inquired at the receptionist's counter then headed for the elevators.

The receptionist had informed me that the woman I needed to see was located on the third floor. Her name was Olwyne Millington and she was in charge of casting.

I could tell that the receptionist had been reluctant to admit someone in my advanced state of inebriation, but I think her sense of humour had kicked in. My appearance at the casting office just might have been preceded by a warning phone call.

The elevator doors opened to expose a large reception area where a stern-looking older woman sat behind a large desk, going through a pile of black-and-white photos. As the doors swished closed behind me she raised her head and looked at me as if I was something that had gotten stuck to the bottom of her shoe.

The elevator had been stuffy and I was feeling a bit groggy, so when she asked in a haughty tone, "What can I do for you?" I simply blurted out; "I want to be an actor."

Then I pursed my lips in a "so there!" fashion, took a step backwards, lost my balance and almost fell down.

It was certainly stuffy in that old office and it was making me dizzy. The secretary was starting to look blurry, but I found that if I closed one eye her face cleared up and I could concentrate on what she was saying.

"Do you have a portfolio and head shots?" she asked.

I didn't know what she was talking about, but I told her I didn't have any of that at the moment but that I was sure that I could get some in the near future. She rattled on for some time about other requirements necessary for applicants and then finished by telling me to come back when

I was sober and serious.

I found her attitude offensive and was just about to tell her so when her intercom buzzed and she was summoned into the next room. By the time she returned I had already pushed the down button on the elevator consol, and was preparing to leave. I was a bit hurt by the reception I had been given and was consoling myself with the knowledge that I had been thrown out of better joints than this.

Then I heard a voice behind me. "One moment, sir!" the receptionist said. "Ms. Millington would like to speak with you."

I gave her my "Of course she wants to see me!" look while she escorted me into the inner office, where a small woman in her early forties sat smoking behind a large desk littered with dog-eared scripts.

She nodded in my direction and, in a lovely, soothing British accent, said, "Sit, please."

She said that she had overheard what was occurring in the reception area and was curious to know more. After quizzing me about what I did for a living, she asked me if I had much acting experience. I thought that a little humour was in order, so I told her that once I had been a tree in a school play.

She was not amused, but neither was she deterred, because she handed me one of the scripts, indicated a character and a page, and asked me to read the lines, saying she would cue me.

I wasn't adverse to kinky stuff but this cueing put me off a bit and I told her so. She just laughed and said get on with it.

I closed one eye so that I could read, then gave it my best effort.

When we finished a couple of pages she asked me to stop and then lit a fresh cigarette and sat and stared at me for what seemed like a long time.

I broke the silence. "So how did I do?" I asked.

She threw her head back, inhaled deeply on her cigarette then launched a perfect smoke ring and said, "You were fucking terrible!"

Then, after a short pause, she said, "However that's just what I need. Are you available tomorrow morning?"

I was a little surprised by her proposal and, not wanting to appear anxious or easy, I slurred, "Let me check my schedule."

Then began fumbling in my in my pockets for a little calendar notebook I sometimes carried to keep track of my mares' gestation periods.

I think she realized that I was bluffing because, by the time I finished digging through my pockets and looked, up she was standing in front of me and tucking a piece of paper in the breast pocket of my shirt.

"That's the address, the time and the contact person. Don't be late," she said in a stern, motherly tone.

"So that's it?" I said, stalling and eyeing the big leather couch against the back wall of her office.

I guess she had seen some of the same movies about the Hollywood star system that I had because she gave me that 'You are a naughty boy' look, spun me around and gently shoved me out her office door, saying, "I mean it. Don't be late!"

And so began my acting career.

I wasn't feeling all that robust when I woke up the next morning. I'd been having nightmares and strange dreams.

At least I thought they were dreams until I found the slip of paper Ms. Millington had given me on my bedside table and realized what I had done.

I read the instructions and checked my watch. If I hurried I could still make the appointment on time. But God, my head hurt, and what if it was just a practical joke? They might be trying to get even with me for showing up at the casting office in the condition I was in.

Maybe I shouldn't go, I thought. It would serve her right for doing business with drunks.

Who was I kidding? I had to find out if it was real or not, so I had a quick shower and shave and headed for the downtown location I had been given.

As it turned out, Ms. Millington was pretty good at her job. She had type cast me as a dumb cop.

The wardrobe people got me suited up in a winter motorcycle uniform, slapped some makeup on my face and showed me the couple of lines I would be required to say.

The TV series they were shooting was called *Wojeck*. It starred an actor called John Vernon and was based loosely on the true-life exploits of a Toronto coroner, Morton Schulman. Of course I was too hungover to appreciate what was going on and I wouldn't have known John Vernon from Adam.

Before we started shooting, Vernon asked me to cue him his lines. I was nervous and, after I messed up several times he accused me of being flippant and stormed off to the other side of the set.

Screw him, I thought. *Who needs him, anyway?*

Then I found out who he was and that the couple of lines I had to say were to be delivered to him. As I shared the shot with him I felt cowed, humble and unsure of myself.

As it turned out, my tentative approach was just what the director was looking for. The scene called for the overbearing Wojeck to give hell to a dozy, incompetent cop at a crime scene. I was perfect for the part.

47: The girl from Chicoutimi

They claim that if you can remember the nineteen sixties and seventies you really weren't there. Well, I was there and, although the memories aren't all happy ones, I still remember most of it.

I suppose the fact that I chose alcohol over LSD, magic mushrooms and the host of other drugs being introduced and bandied about accounts for the stuff that is still floating around in the deep recesses of my aging brain.

Most of my friends at the time were into smoking pot and hash. I don't even smoke tobacco, so it made for some uncomfortable moments at parties when joints would come out and every one was expected to sit in a circle and share the disgusting little spit-soaked bundles.

I didn't want to be a party pooper, so I developed a ruse that made everyone think I was taking part. The success of the deception had a lot to do with what I would say. I always tried to appear anxious for a turn, reaching out and saying things like, "Don't Bogart that joint," or, "C'mon, gimme some." When I got it into my hand I would pretend to inhale heavily on it, hold my breath for an extended period of time then turn away so no one could see me exhale, fake a couple coughs then turn around and say, "Good shit man!" It worked every time.

What the hell, it was the age of Aquarius, the world was changing, the streets were full of bead-draped, long-haired hippies dressed in fringed leather vests and tie-dyed moomoos. They played their banjos and auto harps and sang about world peace and free love, demonstrated at every opportunity and looked like they were having a hell of a good time.

I considered myself situated on the periphery of their movement. I wasn't really typical. My hair was merely longish and I had a full-time job.

I also didn't buy into everything they were advocating. I wasn't naive enough to think that a bunch of kids with flowers in their hair would ever be able to slow down the enormous American war machine; however, the free love aspect of the thing did have a certain appeal and it seems that I was not the only one who took the pledge on that basis because, suddenly, the once staid, conservative City of Toronto seemed to be turning into a modern day Sodom and Gomorrah, with gratuitous sex rapidly replacing the handshake as a form of greeting.

It was during the first few months of that growing revolution that my wife at the time decided to take off to parts unknown with our infant son in hand. I supplied the reason: I had been a bit of a rascal.

I'd been roped into marriage at the age of nineteen when the rabbit died, and I guess I felt that I had somehow been robbed of my formative roving years and that that afforded me a certain license. Anyway, as a result, I found myself single, footloose and, on the surface, fancy free. I was not alone in my situation: several male friends had coincidentally also separated or divorced around the same time.

We formed an alliance of sorts, meeting regularly at local bars and drowning our sorrows in booze and allowing an all-too-willing cadre of free-spirited women to cheer us up.

Believe it or not, it's true: you *can* get too much of a good thing, and that was the way I was feeling one Friday night in late summer as I sat with my friends around a large, barrel-shaped bar at the Coal Bin.

We were on our third jug of beer and, with the arrival of the off-duty secretaries from the surrounding office complexes, the place had started to liven up. There had already been a bit of excitement: a university jock had lost all of his front teeth to a single punch from a diminutive philosophy major during a dispute over one of the local lovelies and, for similar reasons, a man at the next table had taken out his lighter and ignited the tie of the man seated next to him.

Just another night at The Coal Bin and, although my friends were still into the madness and were out on the dance floor hoping to cut a weak one out of the herd, I had had enough. I got to my feet and waded through a sea of come-hither glances on my way to the back door.

I pushed the metal bar under the sign that read *Emergency Exit Only* and stepped out into the cool night air. The door slammed closed behind me and that was that. There was no going back. There would be no more easy women for me; I was hanging it up for good.

I stopped to urinate in the dark alley behind the club before walking out to the first well-lit street, then headed south toward the lake. In my inebriated condition I was thinking of making my way to Sunnyside Beach, where I could get some sand between my toes and clear my head.

I made it to Front Street and was about to turn west when the huge granite façade of Union Station loomed up in front of me. I stared at it for a while before it dawned on me that a train trip might add some real sub-stance to my hasty escape plan.

I groped in my pocket for the huge wad of bills I had cadged from the till at the stables before I left for the evening. It had only been partially depleted by my freeloading friends at the bar, so I was solvent and ready for anything.

I entered the enormous marble hall and made my way to a ticket booth. There were a couple of people ahead of me and, while I waited my turn, I had momentary second thoughts about my plan. I was starting to sober up and thinking maybe I should just go home and sleep it off, but I dismissed the idea.

It wasn't that simple. Since I had become single, my little house beside the stable had become party central. Lots of nights I would return home to find the place in full swing and have to fight my way to my bedroom through throngs of people I hardly knew.

I stepped up to the wicket, determined and ready to go. I was slowed down a bit when the clerk asked me where I was headed.

I had to pause a moment- I hadn't thought that one out. "Oh, any-where," I blurted out. "Where's the next train heading?"

He looked at me strangely for what seemed like a long time, then said, "You look like you should go to Montreal, but you better hurry. The train's about to leave."

I peeled a few bills off my wad, grabbed my ticket and took off running for platform #5.

Twenty minutes later I found myself lounging in a reclining chair, peering out of a smoky train window at the lights of Toronto as they dis-appeared.

I dozed for a while, then woke up with a taste in my mouth like the bottom of a canary cage, so I got to my feet and staggered down to the bar car. Hair of the dog seemed to be in order.

I was on my second Comfort and Collins when she appeared.

I turned from staring at my own reflection in a darkened window to discover a pretty, black-haired, twentyish-looking woman sitting by her-self at a table at the opposite end of the bar. I hadn't noticed her arriving.

She had her hair pinned in a tight roll at the back of her head and was wearing a pair of those heavy, horned-rimmed glasses that were fashion-able at the time. I found myself staring at her and caught her briefly re-turn a glance over the top of the dog-eared paperback novel she was reading.

In keeping with my recent vow of celibacy, I turned away and stared out into the darkness, trying to figure out how far I had travelled.

When I finally looked up to catch the eye of the bartender to order another drink, it seemed to be just him and me in the bar now, the girl had gone. He knew what I was drinking, and while he was putting it together, the door to the ladies' room swung open and the mysterious dark haired lady reappeared. But now the glasses were gone and she had let her hair down.

As she sat down we exchanged smiles, and then she opened her book, pretending to read.

As I sat nursing my drink and exchanging furtive glances with her, I realized that she would have no way of knowing why I was being so standoffish—maybe she would think I was gay or maybe, more importantly, because when I heard her speaking to the bartender they conversed strictly in French. She might think me a snobby Anglo.

My new attitude toward women aside, I felt it important to clear the matter up. I called the bartender over and asked him to invite the lady over to my table for a drink and some clarifying conversation. I didn't want any misunderstanding about my sexual preferences and maybe I would, in a small way, be able to bridge the gap between the two solitudes.

The bartender cautioned me that the young lady spoke almost no English, but as I looked up at him and he now appeared to have two heads, I figured that his caution was academic because, after a couple more drinks, I wouldn't be able to understand her in either official language.

After a bit of feigned reluctance, the girl allowed herself to be escorted to my table. After I got unsteadily to my feet to greet them, the bartender took it upon himself to conduct an elaborate introduction.

I jabbered away at her in English for a few minutes while she nodded and smiled, then we reversed the procedure and I nodded and smiled at the beautiful French she was lisping in my direction. Clearly the conversation, however enjoyable on my part, was going nowhere.

That's when the bartender decided to intervene. As he had nothing else to do, he took a seat in the booth next to us and became our interpreter. He seemed to be taken with one of us, and I wasn't sure if it was me or the girl.

Thereafter, as we sped our way toward Montreal, he was our constant companion, facilitating our conversation while I plied him with drinks that he quaffed surreptitiously after checking the aisle for roving conductors.

In what seemed like a matter of minutes we were pulling into Central Station, with plans for the future becoming imperative. Since I had become a little unsteady on my feet, I had to impose on my two new friends to get me off the train and find me some suitable lodgings.

I don't remember much about our arrival and my departure from the train—just hazy snatches of being assisted by the girl and the bartender through what seemed like a long tunnel until we reached the check-in booth of a hotel. From that point until the following day I can't remember anything that happened.

I woke up naked in a huge bed in a luxury suite. Later, I discovered I was in the Queen Elisabeth Hotel.

Before opening my eyes completely, I groped around under the covers to see if I was alone. I felt a little disappointed that the girl from the train wasn't there, but greatly relieved that neither was the bartender.

Then the alarm bells in my head went off and, in a panic, I dragged myself off the bed and started looking frantically around the room for my clothing. I found my jeans hanging over a chair and, praise be to God, my wallet and money were still in my pockets.

Apparently my two new friends had been good Samaritans, getting me to my room then leaving me to my own devices.

I wasn't feeling very well ,so I decided to take my aching head down to the restaurant that the brochures on the desk said was located downstairs, just off the lobby. I needed liquid and lots of it, but there would be no more hair of the dog for me.

As I examined my pale face and bloodshot eyes in the bathroom mirror, I swore my second oath in less than twenty-four hours: no more drinking. I was done with it—it was over with—I would never touch the stuff again.

I took the elevator to the main floor and headed for the restaurant. The place was crowded and there seemed to be only one small table available at the back of the room.

To get there I had to walk past the breakfast buffet. The sickening, greasy smells of overcooked bacon, ham and eggs wafting out of the heated counter were almost too much to bear.

Somehow I managed to get to my table without puking, then hailed a waiter and ordered a large glass of ginger ale. The first glass was followed by several more, and then something happened that I have never been able to explain.

It seemed that the ginger ale was reactivating whatever alcoholic residue remained in my stomach from the night before. My headache was gone and I found myself drunk as a skunk again.

Over the years I have shared the story of this phenomenon with many learned people. but they always say things like, "It couldn't have happened," or "There is nothing in the literature to support it."

I always reply, "Well, if I wasn't drunk again, why did I stagger out of the restaurant and, noticing a horse-drawn carriage parked outside the hotel entrance, immediately go out and engage it, bribe the driver to sit in the passenger seat, then take reins and the whip myself and set off on a wild two hour tour of downtown Montreal?"

Having explored most of the inner core of the city, much to the relief of a traumatized coachman, I decided to go back to my room for an afternoon nap.

The neon lights of a darkened city were casting a dim glow through the hotel window when I was startled out of my slumber by someone tapping me on my shoulder. It was the girl from the train; she must have kept a room key for herself.

"Get up. C'mon; you get up. We must go."

"Go where?" I inquired.

"You gave money, I got tickets, we must go now."

Not wanting to seem overly inquisitive, but conscious of the fact that I did not have a passport and my funds were not inexhaustible, I asked once more, "Where are we going?"

"You know," she purred, "Chicoutimi!"

Before I was really fully awake, I found myself being assisted, almost dragged, out of my room and ushered down to the lobby. where I settled up for my stay. Then she took me back to Central Station.

All the while I was wondering wondering, *Where the hell is Chicoutimi?*

I was still numb as we boarded the train and the conductor escorted us to a small private compartment where the fold down bed was already made up. *A bit presumptuous*, I thought.

I was about to comment on it when the train suddenly lurched ahead, so instead I pushed a crumpled two dollar bill into the conductor's hand and sat back on the bed. As he closed the door he gave me a sly wink.

I knew I was going to have to do a lot of explaining to my little French mademoiselle and it wasn't going to easy, considering the language barrier. I had to make it clear to her that I was not up for any hanky panky. I was fairly confident that I had not forsaken my vows the previous evening at the hotel and was not about to be tricked into anything now.

I was just launching into an explanation that involved more gesture than sound when she put up her hand and stopped me short. Then, reaching into a bulky cloth bag she had been carrying, she pulled out a bottle of wine and two plastic glasses.

I could have simply said no at that point and put a stop to the whole thing, but what appeared out of that bag sort of astonished me and gave me pause.

She was gripping the neck of a stubb green Mateus bottle. How could she have known that that cheap bubbly had been my choice of vino for several years? In fact, I had been collecting the spent bottles for some time in the hopes of one day gluing them together to replicate a fancy screen I had seen made out them at a U of T frat house.

Not wishing to hurt her feelings, I accepted a glass of the pink, sparkling, pop-like stuff and we toasted each other, she whispering a lengthy phrase in sexy French and me with a, "Here's mud in your eye."

I guess the girl was anticipating a long trip because, as we drained that bottle, another appeared out of her bag.

As the train chugged on through the night and the hours passed, we amused ourselves laughing at stories we told each other, even though neither of us understood a word the other was saying. She seemed to be eyeing me expectantly, but I was more concerned with how I was going to get those empty bottles back to Toronto to add to my collection.

I finally started to nod off. I had a headache and a tremendous bout of heartburn, so I thought I better lie down.

Somehow I had to explain to her that I was feeling ill and wanted to be left alone. I resorted to gesture again and that was a fatal mistake.

I cupped her face in my hands and looked directly into her eyes for a moment then released her and with an anguished look on my face touched my aching head then pulled both hands up against my chest, maintaining the same distressed look. I'm not familiar with American Sign Language, but it seems I might have inadvertently conveyed a message of undying love.

She responded instantly with some unseemly advances and, before I realized what was happening, she had me on my back on the bed and was having her way with me.

She was very strong for a girl and there was no way I could offer any active participation. This went largely unnoticed since the violent rocking of the train seemed to be doing all the work anyway.

When I woke up the following morning, the train was creeping to a halt at a mist-shrouded station in the heart of a town I presumed was our destination.

My companion was seated on the side of the narrow bed. She was crying, and when I put my arm around her in a forced effort to comfort her, she pushed me back roughly and mumbled something about going to confession.

That explained the cross that had been dangling in my face during her recent relentless, unwanted assault.

Maybe this standoffishness is a blessing, I thought as I retrieved the clothing that had been ripped off me and tossed around with careless abandon. *Typical. All that abuse and now I'm the bad guy?*

She continued to avoid me for several minutes—not easy in the small, confined area we shared. Secretly, I was looking forward to the inevitable slap in the face that would end our tryst and set me free.

Unfortunately, that didn't happen. Her conscience must have taken hold of her because, still weeping, she suddenly threw herself in my arms and started uttering what I assumed was an apology.

What could I do? I let her lead me from the train and down a few blocks through the centre of town to an old, but well-kept white, clapboard, three-story house. She took a key from under a brick by the door and let us in.

Somehow she made me understand that we were in her parents' house and that they were both away at work somewhere. She didn't need to spend much time making me understand what she was about when she went to another room and then reappeared with a rosary in one hand and a hat in the other. "You stay, I go confession."

I didn't feel very comfortable being left alone in a strange house, but she wasn't gone long, the church apparently being close by. In retrospect, that would have been the ideal time to make my escape but I still wasn't thinking very clearly and didn't really know where I was, so I stayed.

In fact I stayed for three days. During that time, with the help of the few people we met who spoke a little English, I was able to piece together some background on the strange lady from Chicoutimi.

Several months earlier, seeking fame and fortune as a model, she had responded to a bogus advertisement promising work in Toronto. There was no work and she found herself alone and stranded in a strange city.

Somehow, just as the last of her scant money had run out, she met a young, bilingual photographer who hired her as a model. She showed me several photos he had taken of her during that time, mostly in the nude and quite fetching.

They developed a relationship, and shortly after she moved in with him. They lived together for several weeks, and during that time she wrote home to her parents saying she was engaged and looking forward to bringing her fiancé home to meet the family.

When, at some point, she received an invitation to her cousin's wedding back home, she suggested to her photographer friend that they both attend, but he had seemed reluctant. On the eve of what she thought was to be her triumphant return home, he had unceremoniously dumped her.

She took the train home alone and that was when we met. After leaving me at the hotel in Montreal and going to stay at an aunt's house for the night, she came up with a plan that would save her the embarrassment of showing up at home empty-handed. If I was willing, I was to be her photographer's replacement. I guess not knowing that I was a reformed man, she had thought she had better throw in a few fringe benefits as an inducement.

I played along, met her parents and was invited to use a small bedroom on the first floor off the kitchen. There I slept alone during my entire stay, under the watchful eye of her father.

I only had the clothes on my back when I arrived. The weather was getting a little nippy, so I was forced to buy some warmer duds, plus I needed a suit for the wedding.

I played my part at the nuptials and things went off without a hitch except when the man taking the pictures asked my advice concerning, lighting, depth of field etc., I had to fake a coughing fit to get away from him.

It was at the reception after the ceremony that things began to be a little uncomfortable. For the last day or so my presumed paramour, for the life of me I can't remember her name, had been floating meaningful glances in my direction. Now, as we sat at the head table, she was all over me, playfully grabbing my leg or nudging me when I was supposed to clap or laugh at the French-only speakers.

We sat beside the parish priest who had presided at the wedding, and he kept giving me knowing winks. The confessional obviously was not as sacred and confidential as I had been led to believe.

The realization that something more than I had bargained for was afoot occurred when the bride tossed her bouquet. My girl made a leap worthy of a professional basketball player, snatched the flowers out of the air, pulled me into her arms and, at length, redefined the meaning of a French kiss for me.

Later that evening, back at her house, just as everyone was heading to bed, she took me aside and whispered, "I come to you in morning, they still sleep."

That's when I knew I was in real trouble. The lady was getting serious. She had heard the wedding bells and set her cap. Of course, even if I had been receptive, this would have been awkward for me; technically, I was still married to someone else.

And so it was, with the girl from Chicoutimi's best interests at heart, I waited until, in the wee hours of the morning, I heard the whistle of the departing milk train in the distance. Then I slid the window open, gathered my few belongings and took a French leave.

48: Runaways

Ask any old timer who has spent his life around horses and he'll have a story to tell about the horse that spooked and ran away with him. Cowboys, farmers, loggers even retired city milk wagon drivers- they've all had similar mishaps.

When you're breaking in a young horse you expect that it might have a go at taking matters into it's own hands and running off with you. It's only natural; flight is the horse's first line of defense against predators with bucking coming a close second.

It's the unexpected that throws you for a loop, like when that old team of nags that you have been driving through all kinds of scary conditions for several years, for no apparent reason, takes a bad spell and suddenly bolts and drags you and whatever you're riding in down the road at breakneck speeds. If you're lucky you might get them stopped and under control before too much of your rig has rattled to pieces or you are upside down in a ditch.

My father was full of advice about how to handle these situations. "Let the bastards run," he would say, "and when they get tired and start to slow down, whip their asses and keep them going. Drive the buggers 'til they nearly drop. They'll think twice about trying that trick again."

That would have been good advice and if I had been living on the prairies, where my dad had learned his trade, out where he had miles of straight open road or vast areas of open Saskatchewan grassland to work with. But I wasn't.

My stables were situated in a park in the heart of Metropolitan Toronto, and much of the time I had my horses and carriages out on the busy city streets. When things went wrong in that environment, the consequences could be horrible.

Intentionally letting a team run off their fear was not an option. The streets were too full of pedestrians, buses, streetcars and other traffic.

Back in the days when horses were the main mode of transportation in our big cities, traffic fatalities were almost exclusively due to runaway horses. The newspapers at the time were full of accounts of horses running amok and charging through the streets, dragging disintegrating buggies full of women and children. These events were so common that big city policemen were, as part of their training, given special instruction on how to deal with them.

Awards of valour were frequently given to cops and private citizens for successfully intervening and saving the day, but there were just as many stories about men who had died in the attempt. It was a terrible way to die; men were often impaled by pointed shaft ends or wagon tongues, crushed under heavy wooden spoke wheels, or pounded to a pulp under steel-shod hooves.

No, it was no laughing matter, which, when I look back at the times when I found myself in these hazardous situations, is why I wonder why all I can remember are the funny aspects.

For example, there was the time I decided to take my team and democrat buggy along a very busy city thoroughfare to pick up a girl I had been trying to date, at the office building where she worked.

I had been unsuccessful in all previous attempts to get her attention, and was leaning heavily on the shock value of this latest ploy. I figured she would have to be pretty hard-hearted not to respond to what I had in mind.

When she came out of her office at the end of the day, I would be waiting, all spiffed up and sitting, flowers in hand, in a fancy rig behind a pair of prancing horses. You couldn't get more romantic than that.

She had been playing really hard to get, but I figured that, if I could get her into that buggy and back down the road to my stables and bachelor pad, then I might get the green light.

I know it sounds crass, but she had been so unaccountably standoffish that I felt duty-bound to defend my reputation.

When she found me waiting for her, she was still a bit reluctant to join me, but then she saw several of the women she worked with swooning around the horses and looking like they would willingly take her place, she threw caution to the wind and climbed up in the seat beside me.

Yes! My plan was working, and we set off at a brisk trot, heading south on Leslie Avenue, with me brandishing my whip and her clutching her posies.

For the uninitiated to understand what happened next, I will have to digress and explain a bit about the mechanics of horse-drawn vehicles.

Like any other vehicle, it's essential that a buggy should have the means of going forward, backing up and stopping. It's the last of these requirements that I fell afoul of almost immediately.

Without becoming too technical, I should explain that the main component of the stopping apparatus on these horse-drawn vehicles is a device known as a neck yoke. This is a short crossbar of wood perched at the end of the buggy tongue. It's hooked to the horse's collar, and then a series of straps and buckles winds around the horse's butt and causes the vehicle to stop when the horse does.

Therein lay the problem.

I had been so anxious to make a dashing impression on the lady in question that I was a little too exuberant with my whip, so the horses made a bit of an extra-strong lunge forward as we swung on to the main drag and headed for the park.

No problem, I thought, turning and smiling confidently at my companion while hauling back on the reins to slow the team down.

I could tell she was starting to respond to my efforts to woo her, and for a few seconds our eyes met and we stared longingly at each other while I thought fondly of the candles and wine waiting at my tender trap.

But then something went awry. The horses weren't responding to the several sharp tugs I had given on the reins.

When I looked forward to see what was going on, the spell was broken. My ardour melted away and was replaced with panic and cold fear. The leather strap that held the neck yoke to the end of the tongue had snapped, and now there was nothing to stop the buggy crashing into the horse's rear ends, which now it was doing.

Each time it hit the horses, they became more frightened and increased their speed. When I hauled on the reins I just made the buggy slam into the horses all the harder, so all I could do was sit there with the reins held limply in my hands and hope for divine intervention.

Within seconds, the horses were totally out of control and going full tilt down the road, with the buggy periodically slamming into their asses and egging them on.

I knew what could happen and I was consumed with terror, but when I glanced over at my passenger, she seemed oblivious and just sat smiling like she was enjoying the whole thing. She thought this Ben Hur-esque performance was part of my attempt to impress her.

Within a minute or two we were in sight of the entrance to the park, but we were going so fast that I knew that we could never negotiate the turn safely, so I gave the horses their heads and we galloped past.

It was only a short distance to where the road we were on ended at

Eglington Avenue, a large main street, where I knew I would have a bet-ter chance of turning the corner without flipping over, provided I didn't crash into any of the busy traffic that was flying in both directions through the intersection.

Taking the reins in one hand, I swung my arm around my companion and pulled her in as close to me as possible. I needed all the weight on my side of the buggy to keep it from flipping over.

She still seemed very calm, and even snuggled in closer than I had in-tended. She still had no idea of the danger we were in, and I guess she was assuming I was trying to get to second base.

We hit the corner at breakneck speed, with sparks flying from the horse's shoes, the steel wheels of the buggy skidding sideways on the tarmac, and petals and leaves flying from my passenger's bouquet.

I guess somebody up there likes me, because we made it around the corner and fate provided a large gradual incline on the road in front of us.

Now I was able to pull on the reins without the buggy hitting the horses, and gradually I got them to slow down and we eventually stopped.

I made a temporary repair to the neck yoke with a bit of wire I had in the buggy, and with me still badly shaken, we took an alternate route back to my stables.

God does punish the wicked because, as the evening wore on and we shared each other's company, the lady, so impressed and stimulated by the events of the afternoon, became totally compliant and was ready to grant me my every wish.

I, however, was so shaken, stressed, and traumatized that I was not able to reciprocate in any meaningful fashion.

49: The island

Graham Gower and his wife, Joan, two clients of mine, owned a beautiful little island in Georgian Bay. It was about half an acre in size, not much bigger than a large house lot in the city. There were a few spruce and birch trees around its rocky perimeter and their rustic clapboard cabin was perched near the centre on a sparse area of grass and gravel. It was located about five miles from the nearest jetty on the mainland and at the mercy of the wind and waves; fortunately, the breezes on the bay were balmy in the summer, and during those months the island was a little paradise.

It was, however, quite small. Graham, a psychiatrist, was claustrophobic and wasn't keen on being that far off-shore. He had been on ships that were torpedoed—not once but twice—while serving in the navy in the North Atlantic.

As his passion for riding grew, he chose to spend less and less time on the water and more with his three horses. He knew he was sacrificing the together-time he once had with his family to cater to his other interests and was riddled with guilt, but, as he put it, it was an 'uncontrollable compulsion'.

Joan, as she always had, chose to spend her whole summer on the island. It was becoming a problem. The couple were spending less and less time together and it was putting a strain on their relationship. The island was a two-hour car drive, plus an additional hour boat cruise, from the stable, much too long for a daily commute.

The matter came to a head early one summer when Graham was given the ultimatum: "Me or the horses." Joan had had enough, and Graham was riding the horns of a dilemma instead of one of his regular mounts.

He apprised me of the situation during one of his middle-of-the-night phone calls, and when he asked me if I thought it would be possible to get one of his horses out to the island, I thought, *This time he's really lost it!* I really wasn't prepared to deal with another of his mad schemes at that hour of the morning, so I told him to take a Valium and call me in the morning.

Next morning, when he woke Andrea and me up, as he often did, with cups of tea, he was still going on about his crazy idea.

"It's the perfect compromise," he said. "What could be better? Joan gets to stay on the island and I get to spend the time with one of my horses. Tell me honestly: do you think we can really do it?"

"What do you mean, we?" I said.

"Well, obviously I'll need your help," he replied in a hurt tone.

I could tell that any resistance on my part would be useless at this point, so I attempted to throw up a few logistical roadblocks. "I don't know, Graham. To begin with, we would need a really large barge or scow. Maybe you should check and see if there is anything like that available in the area."

I thought I had him when several days passed and he didn't bring the subject up again. Then I woke one morning to see him smiling over a steaming cup of tea and bursting with the news that he had located a barge that belonged to a construction company and that they were willing to rent it, and a motor boat to tow it. Normally the barge was used to take building supplies to the various islands in the bay but, for a price, they were willing to try their hand at livestock transportation.

Graham was by now obsessed with the idea and money did not seem to be a consideration, so I hit him where I knew it would hurt. "This sort of thing could be very traumatic for your horse, you know. We might cause him permanent psychological damage!"

He was, of course, taken aback and embarrassed that he, of all people, had not considered this very important aspect of the project, and when we parted I thought I had put an end to the matter.

When he returned the following day with a bottle of a new kind of horse tranquilizer, I knew I was trapped so we settled down to plan in earnest.

Job one was to present the plan to his wife Joan, and I drew the short straw. He had already tried and had met with a certain amount of resistance. He explained that she was concerned that the cottagers on the neighbouring islands already considered their family a little eccentric and she did not want to spend her summer explaining why they had a huge horse perched on their postage-stamp-sized atoll. She, unlike her husband, had her feet firmly planted on the ground and was not easy to manipulate.

I told her that the chances of actually getting the horse out to the island were slim and that Graham would probably settle down and see reason before we went ahead with the plan. If, I told her, we actually did bring the horse to her summer sanctuary, the project would be handled in a manner that would not bring any more embarrassment than was absolutely necessary to her and her family.

She reluctantly agreed and I was the only one who hoped more than she did that Graham would forget his crazy obsession.

There was no stopping him, so the plan was set in motion. We booked a horse trailer, and a driver for the large sedan that would pull it, confirmed a time with the man who operated the lumber barge and began to assemble a collection of restraining devises that might prove useful.

I enlisted the help of my old friend Ron Bond, enticing him with the prospect of a weekend on the island, I was sure that another pair of hands would come in handy before the trip was over.

We set out from the city early one morning, making sure that we had adequate time to rendezvous with the barge and boat at the arranged time. Graham had brought along his weekend supply of beer and liquor, and since we had a driver and were about to embark on a dangerous mission, we agreed that a little fortification was in order, so made an early start on Graham's cache of booze.

In truth, I really was dreading what might happen. I even talked Graham into taking his least favourite horse with him in case something went horribly wrong. A couple of drinks were just the thing to ease the tension.

As the three of us sat pondering what might happen when we tried to load the horse on the barge, and both my companions started showering me with what-ifs as if I did this sort of thing every day, I eased my annoyance with several more drinks and they followed suit.

As a consequence, as we arrived dockside, stepped out of the car and breathed in the fresh air blowing in off the bay, our moods were joyous and confident. Except for Ron, who had passed out.

I staggered over to the barge, piped myself aboard and started to inspect the craft. It wasn't quite what I had expected: a huge, rusty, metal affair about thirty feet long and ten feet wide; it looked like a miniature aircraft carrier with a smooth flat steel deck and no sides. The top, which was about six feet above the water line, more or less lined up with the dock, but, as I stepped aboard and felt my feet slipping out from under me, I realized that the horse, who was shod with smooth steel shoes, would never be able to walk aboard, let alone stand, while we towed him five miles over the choppy waters of the bay.

I returned to where Ron and Graham were waiting, bearing my bad news and secretly rejoicing that we would have to abandon the project, but they had broken into a bottle of Bacardi and were busy celebrating the successful completion of the land portion of the journey and were in no mood to listen to my defeatist concerns.

We invited the captain of our set of crafts to join us in a tactical discussion, but, as we shared the rum and pondered the matter of the slippery deck, no solutions were immediately forthcoming. Our problem-solving ability was diminishing with the level of hooch left in the rum bottle.

That's when inspiration struck. I had been watching some people preparing to go snorkelling on the beach beside our dock and remembered the two sets of flippers that Ron had brought along in his kit of beach toys for the weekend.

My mind drifted back to the days when the mounted unit first started providing a mounted guard at the new city hall in Toronto. We had encountered a similar problem to, the one we now faced: the super-smooth concrete of Nathan Philips Square was too slippery for the normal horseshoes we used, so we substituted rubber ones and the problem was solved.

I didn't have any rubber horseshoes, but I did have Ron's two sets of flippers.

"The flippers! We have the flippers!" I exclaimed.

"Impossible!" Graham slurred, "the horse could never swim that far."

"No, No, No," I stuttered, then went on to explain about the police horses.

"What exactly are you proposing!' Graham burped, his interest sparked.

"That I use the leg bandages that we brought with us to tie the flippers onto the horses' feet. If I can get them on securely, they will work like rubber shoes."

"Sounds perfectly reasonable to me," blurted the captain.

Since Ron had passed out again, I figured I had a consensus and started digging through our chest of special supplies.

I experimented at length with the positioning of the flippers and finally settled on a configuration whereby, on the front feet, the webbed portion of the flipper jutted out in front of the horse and, on the back feet, that portion stuck out behind. After a major panic and a little practice, I managed to get the horse flipflopping along the beach, and I decided to add the other precautionary equipment we had brought along to ensure the horse's safety.

A crowd of curious people had begun to gather as I fitted the Standard Bred racing goggles, with blinkers, on the horse's head, saddled him, and attached the two large truck inner tubes on either side.

He looked a bit like a sea serpent, and we were quite a sight as we made our final test run along the beach; the horse trotted along with his head held high, squinting through the goggles, flippers flopping and tires flapping.

Many of the people in the crowd were Graham's neighbours and fellow island owners, and I heard a lot of laughing and some unkind remarks being murmured.

All was now in readiness. A pail of oats sat on the barge to use as an enticement should the horse balk when we tried to load him, and a syringe of tranquilizer was ready to be administered.

I tied the horse near the end of the dock, and we all decided that another drink was in order to fortify us for the voyage ahead and before we undertook the difficult task of getting the horse on the barge. We knew it was bound to be the most challenging part of the exercise and there was quite a bit of debate about how it should be handled.

One drink led to another, and the sequence only stopped when the captain cocked a weather eye and suggested that we get on with the job, because the waves were getting bigger by the minute.

We gathered our resolve and, with a vow to manhandle the beast onto the boat if necessary, proceeded to where I had left the horse tied.

But the horse was gone.

In a panic, we turned and scanned the beach, expecting to see a madly flip-flopping horse disappearing in the distance.

After a moment Ron, who had temporarily regained consciousness, tapped me on the shoulder and pointed toward the barge. There, in the middle of the craft, stood our horse, with his nose buried in the pail of oats, quietly munching away. The horse had obviously grown tired with our endless debate over how to load him and taken matters into his own hands.

"Clever lad! Clever lad!", shouted Graham.

I hurried aboard and held the horse's head while the rest of the crew finished loading our gear and casting off the lines. The captain's boat tightened the tow-line and we began tacking into the wind.

I hoped that the rest of the trip would be smooth sailing, but that was not the case, not even close. For one thing we had forgotten to administer the tranquilizer, and the crew were the only ones sedated.

For some reason, I was the only one who ended up on the barge with the horse. Graham and Ron chose to ride in the towboat with the captain. They did however shout encouragement to me when we left the protected harbour and the waves became larger and more frequent.

The craft began to rock and pitch, and the horse instinctively assumed a spread-eagled stance and braced himself. He was faring better than I was, so I moved to the centre of the deck and joined him, and that's how we spent the remainder of that terrible voyage, leaning on each other, him occasionally neighing and me constantly praying.

I have never been a sailor; I have always been nervous on open water. When I began to sober up and realize my predicament, I began to panic.

Fortunately, the horse was cool, calm and collected and was the source of solace that got me through, I guess I was the one who should have been wearing the blinkers and inner tubes.

After what seemed like an eternity, we reached some calmer water near Graham's island and slowly approached his small dock. The horse was still calm, but I was pawing the deck and chomping at the bit, anxious to abandon ship.

When we were about a hundred yards from the dock, the tow boat stopped suddenly, threw the outboard into reverse and headed back toward the barge. As he drew alongside, the captain shouted that he couldn't bring me any closer because the water was too shallow.

He cast off the tow line and stood off at a distance, leaving me to figure out what to do. I sure as hell didn't want to make the return trip to the mainland with the horse. I could see whitecaps forming on the waves on the open water beyond the shelter of the island.

I knew I had only one chance, and I used the last trace of liquid courage in my system to force myself to remove the horse's goggles, shove an inner tube out of the way, and vault into the saddle. I gathered the reins, dug my heels into the horse's flanks, and yelled as loudly as I could.

For the first time since we started the trip, the horse actually was startled. He took two strides forward, then hurled himself off the barge and into the water.

It was like riding Pegasus for about a second. Then we hit the water, and everything fell to pieces, literally, The inner tubes ripped off and took me with them; the flippers seemed to work for a second or two, then dislodged and floated to the surface.

I managed to grab the horse's tail and held tightly, using it as a rudder to steer him toward a small sandy beach as I clambered back into the saddle.

The horse arrived on the island unscathed, but it took the rest of the weekend for me to recover.

The horse spent the rest of the summer on the island, and peace reigned in the Gower family. When the time came for the horse to be removed from the island, a task that would require an expensive lengthening of the dock and major improvements to the barge, I arranged to be out of the country.

50: The Augean

Where there are horses there is bound to be horse manure, there's no avoiding it. One of the first problems I encountered when I started my riding school was disposing of the stuff.

My stable was located in a park in the heart of Toronto and, for a time, the mushroom growers on the outskirts of the city were willing to haul the dung away at no charge. That arrangement didn't last very long, however. The Health Department intervened, demanding that all of the refuse from my barn, and others in the city, be contained in sanitary bins that would be required to be removed and replaced several times a week.

It was an expensive proposition and I immediately began to try to figure out a way around it.

I was stumped for quite a while until one day, when I was eating my lunch in the kitchen and listening to the TV blaring away in the living room. Johnny Mathis was singing the theme song to the cartoon series "Hercules." I didn't mind the song, or the show, but when that annoying little centaur named Newton started screeching, "Herc! Herc!' I couldn't stand it anymore and started down the hall to turn the set off.

That's when it hit me!

I remembered the stories of the trials of Hercules, and in particular the one about his task of cleaning out the massive Augean Stables. As I recalled, it was the fifth task that King Eurystheus set for him. He had only one day to muck out an enormous barn.

At first, the job had seemed impossible, but, true to form, Hercules came up with a solution. He bashed holes through opposing walls of the stable, diverted a river to flow through the openings and, voilà! the poop was gone.

The wheels began to turn. My first thought (immediately dismissed) was that I might make use of the Don River; it flowed by only a few yards from my barn. But, no, I had to be practical, and it wasn't until I was seated in a location where some of my most inspired thoughts come to me that I found the perfect solution.

Actually, it happened immediately after I flushed and was listening to all that water gurgling down the drain.

My barn had recently been hooked up to the city's sewer system, so why not create a toilet for the horses, too? Yes, that was it.

It wouldn't really be a toilet. The intense training I would have to put the horses through would make that prohibitive. No, what I had in mind was an immense flushing system that would carry the manure away from behind the horses' stalls and flush it down the city's drain.

The barn had originally been designed to house dairy cattle and, as a consequence, had gutters running along behind the stalls. When we converted the space for horses we simply planked them over. As my plan began to develop I realized that these cement flumes could be an important component of the flushing system I was proposing.

My final plan (and I use the term loosely because I never really plan anything; I just start doing it and allow it to happen) was to cut access holes into the gutter behind the horses and install a series of high pressure water nozzles to drive the manure out of the barn and into the sewer.

The actual feces would not pose a problem, but I knew that the straw I used to bed the horses would probably clog up the system, so I didn't even try to use it. The ideal bedding would have been fine sawdust, but none of that was available, so I decided to try wood chips.

I located what I needed in Quebec and had a boxcar load shipped in.

It took me a couple of weeks of tinkering to get ready, but finally I had the horses standing in the sweet- smelling shavings and all systems were a go. I opened the main water valve and the stable men started shovelling the manure into the gutter.

Wood chips and dung began flowing toward the entrance to the sewer, where I had placed a battery of super-high-pressured nozzles to whisk the slurry on its way. It was working like a charm, and in half the time it normally took to muck out the stables we were finished and congratulating ourselves.

We settled in to using the system twice a day, and I was so proud and pleased with myself that I went next door to the police stable to try to talk Inspector Johnson into using my invention.

About a week later, I was sitting in my kitchen pondering the possibility of patenting my idea, when a man in city uniform appeared at my door. He was very polite about it, but he informed me that he and his crew were busy trying to unclog a section of sanitary sewer line approximately two miles in length. He said that the offending matter appeared to be horse manure and wood chips and wondered if I knew anything about it.

While I remained silent, trying to formulate a suitable lie, he went on to say that if his crew had not found and relieved the blockage in time, it might have bunged up half the toilets in North York. The evidence was pretty compelling, so I decided to 'fess up and throw myself on his mercy.

After a long conversation and a commitment to give free riding lessons to each of his four grandchildren, we were back to shovelling shit... but I heard no more about it.

51: Lady Godiva

In the nineteen seventies, horses were becoming an oddity in the streets of Toronto. Whenever a horse-drawn vehicle or a mounted policeman made an appearance, they would draw everyone's attention. I recognized the potential that my horses and antique wagons had as an advertising tool and started contacting various agencies around town. Because my stables were located in the heart of the city, I was well positioned to respond quickly to the many requests that started coming in.

Once the word got out, I was kept busy promoting various products and events, and each one was a new and interesting challenge. I or one of my assistants, in addition to supplying the horses, was often required to appear in strange costumes and regalia, as a knight in full armour riding his charger up and down Bloor Street, a centurion driving a chariot around the parking lot of a shopping mall, or a Governor General's Horse Guard trooper standing guard at the entrance to the ball room on the fifth floor of the Royal York Hotel. I never knew what I was going to be asked to do, but if the price was right, I never said no.

One day a unisex hair salon that wanted to promote their grand opening approached me. I met with the two flamboyant new owners and they laid out their plans for me.

"Picture this!" one of them said, touching his forehead with the back of hand and staring off into the distance. "A nude Lady Godiva, mounted on a pure white horse and led by a handsome page in period costume, walking up Younge Street right to the door of our salon."

"I can make the page's costume!" the other owner chimed in, "I already have a set of tights."

"Well gentlemen," I said, "I suppose it's possible. I do have a white horse that would probably meet your requirements, but the matter of the page might prove difficult. I don't think I will be able to talk my assistant into wearing those tights you're talking about, and I am damned sure I'm not going to do it."

"Not a problem!" they sang out in unison. One of them continued, "We already have a page lined up, a friend of ours. He knows all about horses."

"Yes!" confided the second man, "and I hear he's hung like one!"

Whereupon they both started tittering uncontrollably.

A buck's a buck, I said to myself as I booked the date. The only thing I was concerned about was the page's ability to manage the horse, but my two clients reassured me that Clark, as they called him, had lots of experience and that I was not to worry. I don't know why, but I took them at their word and let the matter drop.

The only pure-white horse I had was a spirited gelding. He was quite obedient and controllable if you knew what you were doing, but if he thought he could get away with it he would get a bit trying at times. I had rented him out on the 12th of July a couple of times and Constable Mo Clarke, dressed up as King Billy, seemed to get along with the horse fairly well as he led the Orange Lodge's annual parade through the heart of the city.

When the day arrived for the salon promotion, we trucked the horse to the store and were greeted by Lady Godiva and her loyal page. She was a buxom young lady, cleverly clad in a skin-coloured body stocking that, on first glance, made her appear nude. Her long blonde hair covered just enough of her ample breasts to keep the morality squad at bay.

The effect was quite good; I know it worked for me.

The page was a different matter. I had begun to sense a problem when I saw him striding down the front steps of the beauty parlour clad in yellow leotards, green pantaloons, a white lacy top and a puffy purple hat with a large feather. He seemed to float in my direction as I stood by the horse's head.

I began to be further concerned when I introduced him to the horse. His eyes were wide with fright and it seemed to take all of his courage to force himself to come close enough to give the horse a limp-wristed pat on the neck.

Glancing around to see that nobody was looking in our direction, he clutched my wrist and, leaning forward, whispered in my ear, "You know, don't you?"

I looked perplexed; I wasn't sure what he meant.

He winked at me and said, "About the horse, silly! This is the closest I've ever been to one."

I should have known better. I was constantly running into the same problem: desperate young actors and performers willing to swear to anything to get a job.

"I don't think you will be able to handle this beast," I told him, "Why in hell would you lie about something like this? You could get yourself killed."

"I know!" he replied. "But I needed the money. I'm a ballet dancer and I haven't worked for a while."

I may have looked a little pissed off, because he turned to me with a hurt look on his face and suggested the unimaginable, "Say, you're about my size. Why don't you take my costume and lead the horse yourself?"

This put the situation into a whole new light. Not that there was anything wrong with it, but there was no way they were getting me into those tights.

I was frantically trying to think of a way that I could make the original plan work when I remembered a small, amber coloured bottle of liquid that might still be in my truck.

I led the horse over and, leaning through the open window on the passenger's side, opened the glove compartment. Thank God it was still there, complete with syringe and needle.

About two weeks earlier, a mare of mine was acting up on a movie set. She had been filmed several times previously during the production and it was essential for the sake of continuity that she be in the scene that was causing her to panic.

I contacted Paul Cairnes, an ex-cop in his last year of Vet school, and he suggested I try a new horse tranquilizer called Atrivet. It had worked wonders, transforming my crazy mare into a docile pussycat. I was sure that this stuff was the magic elixir that would keep me out of those tights. I injected a hefty dose of the drug into the white gelding's neck and he immediately started to relax.

While we waited for the full effect, I gave the page a quick lesson on how to lead a horse without getting his toes broken. He seemed more at ease; apparently he had fortified himself with some liquid courage while I was attending to the horse.

I hadn't had time to read the lengthy instructions on the label of the drug bottle concerning how long it would last or any side effects to expect, so, when the horses' eyes started to get droopy I decided we best be on our way.

We hoisted the semi-naked lady on to her sidesaddle and, after she adjusted her hair, we set off down the street. I walked beside the page for a few yards, then, as we started to get the attention of the people on the sidewalks, I decided that it would be better if I followed discreetly along the curb, pretending I didn't know them.

I guess the page hadn't lied about his ballet experience. Rudolph Nureyev couldn't have done a better job of strutting and playing to the crowd.

Anyway, I could see that the page was in control of the situation and the old horse was just following along behind him, yawning and trying to stay awake, so I decided to stop and get a coffee in a café along the way. The entourage wasn't moving that fast; I could catch up later.

By the time I finished my coffee, my charges were out of sight and I had to jog a bit to catch up. In the distance I could hear laughter, honking horns, whistles and the general hum of crowd noise.

I could see Lady Godiva's head bobbing above the throngs of people who had now gathered around her, so I knew she was still safely mounted and making her way down the street.

When I crossed to the other side of the street to get a better look I couldn't help laughing myself. I didn't know at the time, but the tranquilizer I had administered had a peculiar side effect on geldings.

Lady Godiva, elated and haughty, was obviously being inspired by the crowd and the page was striding along even more heroically than when he began, playing to an appreciative audience.

What they both didn't realize was that, due to the effects of the tranquilizer, the gelding's penis was hanging flaccid and fully extended below him; a two-foot-long truncheon swaying rhythmically back and forth in time with the page's paces.

I decided to leave well enough alone.

The grand opening was well attended. I had conducted one of the most effective advertising campaigns ever!

52: Cinderella

I never imagined anybody would ever get me decked out in leotards and pantaloons, but that was before something that occurred just before Christmas in 1972.

Earlier in the fall I had committed myself to supplying a pony for a British pantomime called *Cinderella*. It was to be performed at Eaton Auditorium.

It had been explained to me that 'pantomime' was a British traditiion, a type of show, always performed around Christmas, that took a fairy tale as its theme, added music and dance and reversed the roles of the players so that men would be playing the women's parts and vice versa. It sounded a little kinky for Brits, but who was I to judge?

They needed a pretty, silver, dappled pony with a white mane and tail to pull Cinderella's carriage onstage. When they told me what they were willing to pay for the use of the pony and its handler, ignoring the fact that I currently did not own a pony of that description, I recklessly agreed to supply the said animal.

When December 5 rolled around, and I got a call from the producers telling me that they were starting rehearsals in two weeks, I still hadn't sourced out a suitable pony. There were lots of quiet ponies to be had—pintos, bays, blacks, greys even appaloosas—but no silver dapples with white mane and tale.

The weekly horse auction at Kitchener Livestock Sales, northwest of the city, might have been my last chance to find what I needed.

I had walked past almost all of the critters lined up for the auction and was losing hope when I noticed movement in pen in a dark corner of one of the out-buildings. I looked over the top rail, and there in the gloom was the pony I was looking for.

At least I thought he was until he suddenly bared his teeth, reared up and lunged at me. I shot backwards as his teeth snapped shut about an inch from my nose.

I guess I'll pass on you, pal, I thought, moving away to check for more suitable candidates

Unfortunately, there seemed to be an unusual dearth of silver dapple ponies in the region that day. It was back to the pony from hell.

When the pony came up for sale I was hoping none of my associates would notice me when I raised my hand at a ten dollar bid and the auctioneer said, 'Sold.' All the boys around the stockyards stood watching and scratching their heads as I drove off, with the pony screeching defiance, rearing, and almost kicking the tailgate off.

With the help of my dad and two stable workers we got him safely off my truck and incarcerated in a sturdy box stall. I knew I had to get the little demon broke and quieted right away.

To everyone's surprise, including mine, after a few intense days, my improvised techniques to convince him that he shouldn't kill me began to work and the pony began to settle down. With any luck, I would have him harness broken and ready to go to work when the rehearsals for the pantomime started.

Two weeks later, Lucky was a changed beast and I had him pulling a cart around the park roads. He wasn't perfect; I knew he would still need a firm hand to control him when he made his début at the theatre, but he had come a long way.

The trouble was that, when I turned him over to a handler whom I wanted to take over the job, the pony reverted to his evil former self. He started rearing, biting and kicking and wouldn't stop until I took over again. Apparently his new good manners hinged on my presence, and there wouldn't be enough time to establish a new relationship.

I was in for it. I would have to handle the pony during the run of the show.

Eaton Auditorium was a large theatre located on the top floor of a famous old, multi-leveled department store at the corner of Young and College streets in downtown Toronto. It was a beautifully designed room, with vaulted ceilings, crystal chandeliers and ornate Art-deco décor.

Timothy Eaton had failed to notice the absence of one important feature when he signed off on the architect's plans for the place. There was no freight elevator leading to the theatere on the top floor.

It was an oversight that I only became aware of when my pony and I arrived at the location for the first rehearsal. The only way to get to the top floor was to use the bank of elevators that served to move the store's regular clients from level to level.

In his defence, old Timothy in his wildest dreams could not have anticipated the necessity of hoisting a pony up to his beautiful theatre.

After a hurried meeting with the show's producers and the store management, I was informed that I would be permitted to lead the pony across the main floor of the store and use one of the elevators located on the back wall.

My most direct avenue to the elevators would see me beginning my passage in the ladies' lingerie department, passing through the area where jewellery was displayed, and ending at millinery, just in front of the elevators.

I approached my first trip through the store with the pony with a certain amount of trepidation. I was about to try to lead the pony that had terrorized the Kitchener Stockyards two short weeks earlier through a crowd of women buying corsets and trying on hats.

That's when we encountered our first problem; the entrance was equipped with a revolving door. I was stymied for the moment, so I just stood there eyeing the contraption for possibilities…

Finally I looked up to see the store manager staring through the window at me with an incredulous look on his face and pointing in the direction of a set of regular doors located further down the block.

We got into the store with very little trouble, and as the pony and I wove our way through the aisles of glitzy merchandise I tried to appear nonchalant. Everything went much better than I expected. No one screamed or ran for the exits and we reached the elevator banks without any further trouble.

I pressed the up button, then the pony and I stood a discrete distance back from the sliding door while we waited our turn. Moments later the doors of our lift swished open, and a rather startled group of women emerged, clutching their shopping bags and giving us wide berth.

As Lucky and I started forward, a stern-looking older lady elevator operator assumed a defensive position in the centre of the door, effectively blocking our entrance. However, when she got the nod from the store manager, who had been hovering nervously in the background, she acquiesced and reluctantly let us aboard.

She was just about to close the doors when two women rushed forward and attempted to join us. The operator tried to deter them, but they insisted that they had seen the cute pony and would be delighted to share the elevator with us.

At Eaton's the customer was always right, so we became a party of five and began our ascent.

The two women immediately began fawning over Lucky, talking baby talk to him and patting him with their white-gloved hands. Surprisingly, he didn't seem to mind the attention.

Then something terrible happened. He suddenly dropped his head and coughed violently, and in the same instant lifted his tail and let a thunderous fart.

It was only a matter of seconds 'til we reached the next floor, where the ladies, making a hasty, unscheduled evacuation, burst through the elevator doors and disappeared, gasping and gagging, into fourth floor china.

The old elevator operator wasn't too excited about getting back into the car, but after she waited awhile for the air to clear she climbed aboard, and we resumed our trip to the top floor.

I had been so preoccupied with getting the pony ready for the show that I hadn't thought much about the way things would be backstage. By the time we arrived the place was a hive of activity. The band was warming up in the orchestra pit and a dozen or so ballerinas were swirling around in tutus and toe shoes, waiting their turn to perform.

I reluctantly left the pony in the stall I had improvised for him, guarded only with a 'beware of pony' sign, while I was ushered away to be fitted out in the dreaded leotards, pantaloons and curled toe shoes.

When my ordeal was finally over and got back to the pony, the warning sign I had pinned to the stall was lying in shreds on the floor, and all the children dancers who were there to perform an excerpt from the *Nutcracker Suite* were clustered around. The pony was munching on something and I hoped it wasn't a set of tiny fingers. As it turned out one of the kids was sharing her oatmeal cookie with him.

My warnings to them fell on deaf ears, and during the run of the show, every time I turned my back the little pixies and the other ballet dancers were back at it again, feeding and pampering him.

To my surprise, when I led him, pulling Cinderella's carriage, onto a stage full of flouncing dancers with the band blaring away and the audience applauding, he didn't even flinch.

Everything went well after that except that, as they are wont to do, the production company went bankrupt and I didn't get paid.

As I led the placid pony back through the store on the way home, I reasoned that we both had had a valuable lesson.

53: The mystery of the blue roan pony

As I checked out the line of ponies tethered to the rail in the long low barn at the Kitchener Horse Auction, a little blue roan gelding with a black face and matching legs caught my eye. He was well built and about the size I needed for my riding school.

I went in for a closer look, ran my hands over him and checked his mouth. He must have come from a good home because, unlike the other ponies, he was well groomed and had a red ribbon braided in his mane.

The old saying is that "If it looks too good to be true, it probably is", so I had learned to be very careful. I untied the pony, took him out of the barn and hopped on his back, expecting the worst. To my surprise, he was a real little gentleman and went through his paces without a hitch.

He even neck reined, responding easily to the touch of the halter rope.

I made up my mind that I had to have him.

The auctioneer, sensing my interest, showed no mercy, and I ended up paying the premium price of thirty dollars for him. (Ponies were a dime a dozen back in the 1970s.)

When I got him home, I put him right to work. The riding instructors fitted him out with a little English saddle, and for several days he earned his keep while the kids in the junior classes posted around on his back.

It was about two weeks later when I noticed something peculiar about him. I'd agreed to rent him out to some parents who wanted a pony to lead around. We used different tack for that job: fancy little western saddles with a horn for the kids to hang on to.

I was in the barn and Dick, my stableman, had the new pony out in the paddock getting him ready when I heard a group of kids burst out laughing. I went out to investigate.

Dick was trying to tack up the pony and wasn't having much luck. When he placed the saddle blanket on the animal's back and then turned to reach for the saddle, the pony would swing his head back, grasp the blanket in his teeth, snap it off his back and toss it to the ground. This had happened several times and the kids were getting quite a kick out of the pony's performance.

I went out and held the pony's head while Dick finished getting him ready, and once he was tacked up the little imp didn't give anybody any further trouble.

The pony's antics were unusual but seemed harmless, so I didn't think much more about him until a week later.

Dick had given me a list of the horses and ponies that needed their feet trimmed, and the new roan pony was first in line. It was a nice day, so I decided to work outside. While I strapped on my leather apron and gathered up my tools, Dick led the pony into the paddock and held him.

I approached the pony and leaned over to pick up his near forefoot and, as I did, my hand touched his elbow.

The pony immediately bent one knee and dropped into a perfect bow.

At first I thought he was trying to avoid having his feet trimmed, but when he bent his head down with his forehead touching the ground, I figured there must be something more going on.

He stayed in that position for quite a while, glancing up at me out of the corner of his eye as if trying to tell me something.

I finally clued in, trying to find the signal to get him back on his feet. Finally I said, "Up!" and he did just that, leaping to his feet and shaking the sand off his nose.

Dick and I were both intrigued by what the pony had done, so we put off the hoof trimming while we investigated further.

I led the animal to the centre of the riding ring, where there was lots of soft sand, to see if I could get him to repeat his performance. No problem. I touched the same elbow and the pony bowed again.

We repeated it several times to make sure it wasn't a fluke and then I decided to try something else. Reaching over his back, I touched the far elbow at the same time as the one closest to me and—voila!—he went down on both knees. We did that a few times and then I decided to up the ante.

While he was down on both knees I tried to get him to bend his hind legs and go all the way belly down to the ground. I was a while exploring his body, pressing, squeezing and imploring, but finally I found the magic spot on his rump and he obligingly plopped down.

From that position it was easy to get him to roll over or to lie upside down with all four feet in the air. After we got to know each other better, he would let me sit astride his upturned belly and pump his legs up and down.

Dick and I realized that we had a trick pony on our hands, and over the next few weeks we both learned more and more about his capabilities.

He was a real hit with my clients, and one day, when I had him in the ring performing, I unknowingly gave him a signal that initiated his best previously-undisclosed trick.

I was standing directly in front of him and, for some reason, I raised both of my arms at the same time, like Moses parting the waters.

Tricksy, as we now called him, reared up on his hind legs and shuffled, stiff-legged, towards me.

I was a little shocked and took a couple of steps backwards, but when I did, he followed, still walking on his hind legs. He seemed to expect me to stay still so that's what I did.

He moved in on me until my nose was touching his breastbone and his legs were draped over my shoulders.

One of the kids shouted, "He looks like he wants to dance!" and, as it turned out, that's exactly what he had in mind.

As he hung almost weightless over my shoulders, he let me spin him around in a weird waltz.

Over the following months, I learned more and more about the little blue pony's marvellous abilities. I could get him to answer yes by nodding or no by shaking his head to and fro to questions I put to him. Sometimes I would get him to tell the kids his age by pawing the ground with his hoof. I arranged it so that he would stop at two or three years so that I could then say, "C'mon, Tricksy, be honest," and then he would give me a peeved look and start scratching madly away at the ground until I told him to stop.

Of course there were lots of secret signals necessary to get him to perform these tricks, but circus lore prohibits me from divulging them!

I would have taken Tricksy with me when we moved to the Maritimes, but the men buying my business made leaving him a condition of the sale.

All of that was a long time ago, but when I go through my old photo albums and see a picture of the little blue pony, I start thinking afresh about Tricksy's mysterious life before we met. I was never able trace his previous owner.

It could have been a young girl heading off to college, but more probably was an old horse trainer like myself who had taken the pony on as a swan song project before he made his last trip to the stables.

54: Escape to the country

It's ironic that, just a short time before all of this happened, I was still a policeman with aspirations of becoming a detective, and couldn't have imagined that my crafty old farmer father would be able to upstage me and expose and help solve a major crime on his own.

In the spring of 1970, I decided that a summer residential riding school would be a good way to expand my riding academy business. I found a rental farm a few miles out of the city, converted the dairy barn into horse stalls, built a bunk house, put in a swimming pool and ar-ranged for my dad and mother to live on the place year-round.

It was a good arrangement, and the first year went off without a hitch. Happy campers, satisfied parents of the kids and good returns for the bottom line. The following year was fully booked and, to quote TIMBUK3, "The future looked so bright I thought I might need to wear shades."

Later in the summer, about halfway through the camping season, I got a call from the lawyer who represented the group of developers who owned the property. He wanted to know if I would be amenable to allowing the company to store some con-struction equipment on the

Dad

farm for a short time.

I knew I was getting the place at a bargain rate and didn't want to rock the boat, so I said it would be okay if they found a discrete spot that wouldn't interfere with my riding school, then I let my father know about the arrangement and I never gave the matter a second thought.

The construction equipment, consisting of several huge excavator arms and buckets and an operational backhoe, was shortly trucked over to farm.

Then, in a subsequent conversation, my father said something that I should have paid attention to, but didn't. "Them fellas are always coming up here and fiddling around with the equipment and I can't figure out what they're doing."

"Well, as long as they are not getting in the way, Dad, I wouldn't worry about it," I advised him.

But a couple of weeks later I got a really frantic phone call from him, saying that my brother-in-law, Ray, was up at the farm and saw some men digging a big hole out behind the barn and burying something.

"And so?" I said, still not concerned.

He went on, almost shouting now, "Ray took the backhoe and dug up what they were burying and guess what they found?"

I wasn't in the mood for guessing so I let him go on. "There was a huge aluminum box, about twice the size of a coffin, and it was filled with big blocks of yellow stuff wrapped in plastic."

Now he had my attention, and when I could breathe again, I shouted back at him, "For Christ's sake, call the cops!"

"Your mother already has and —whoops—it looks like they just arrived. Get your ass up here!"

Then he hung up.

Half an hour later, when Andrea and I arrived at the farm, the *Wally Harkness*
driveway was full of police vehicles, bumper to bumper, and cops spilling out all over the property.

As we ducked under the police tape for a closer look, a familiar face greeted me: Wally Harkness, someone I once served with in Toronto. He was famous for recovering the stolen Stanley Cup and had recently been made a detective with York Regional Police.

He showed me over to where the excavation in question lay like an open grave. "What you are looking at," he said, "is, in my estimation, the largest cache of illegal drugs ever uncovered in Canada, and it seems to be in your backyard."

Then he turned to me, all business-like, "What can you tell me about the owners of this property and the guys that buried this stuff?"

I referred them to the lawyer I had signed my lease with. That's all I knew about anybody else involved until the subsequent investigation was done.

The police and the press took their photos and departed, but that wasn't the end of it.

Dad called the following day to say that he hadn't been able to figure out why the huge tubular excavator arms had so many metal patches spot welded on them, then said, "I took a sledgehammer and knocked a couple of them off and guess what? Them damned things are full of the stuff. Probably more than was in that chest we dug up."

Detective Harkness, suitably impressed with my father's detective work, gave me what he termed a courtesy call to fill me in on how his investigation was progressing.

"The four men, who are registered owners of the farm you are renting, all jumped the first plane back to Israel. Interpol tells me that they are all involved in the Israeli Mafia. I didn't know there was one. But here's the thing: the word on the street is that their people who are still in the country are not pleased with you turning them in, so you and your dad better watch your backs."

When I went back to the farm, I told my dad about the warning and he went and brought out his old shot gun and said, "I'd like to see the bastards try something."

I was worried about my parents' safety, and just as worried about what might happen to any prowler who might happen onto the place, so shorty after I packed up my parents' stuff and moved them to a safe place in the city.

I still had to explain to Andrea why, for the rest of the time before we were able escape to our hidden sanctuary in the Maritimes, I would be sleeping next to her with a loaded revolver under my pillow.

And as luck would have it, shortly after we arrived in Nova Scotia somebody stole that very gun. But that's another story.

Getting this newspaper clipping back together was like working on a Dead Sea Scroll.

55: The way we were

My dabbling at police work was meant to be a temporary affair. Just a way to fill in time until I found a more suitable vocation.

The thought of me actually becoming an honest-to-god policeman was laughable. And, as it turned out, there was lots to laugh at. But the short tour of duty that I had planned stretched out into years and, in truth, it wasn't all wasn't fun and games.

Watching things evolve around me from a detached distance, I realize now that I was fortunate to be given a glimpse into an all but forgotten way of policing and serving the community.

Glocks, Tasers, body armour, body cameras, military-type assault weapons and special cell phones had not even been dreamed of when I was first sent out on the beat in the inner city with a rusty old WW1 446 Webley revolver crammed into my holster. Toronto police had just stopped wearing Bobby helmets in 1945.

In addition to my gun, handcuffs and a night stick, I was given the key to the call boxes placed strategically on selected street corners and given a caution to always have sufficient coins in my pocket, should I have to go to a phone booth to report an emergency.

The men—women in uniform were almost non-existent in those days —were almost all white Anglo-Saxons, many of the older men WW2 veterans. The first black man and one woman constable started with me in my second class at the Police College in the early 1960s.

When I joined, I should say was tricked into joining, the Mounted Unit, there were still seven established stables, attached to police stations spread across the city. The horses, in addition to being a back-up for crowd control, were simply another form of transportation to allow constables to go about their regular duties.

Their purpose as a public relations tool has always been underrated. Everybody loved to see the police horses.

It's strange that, as I have reflected on those long-ago days, I have had to dig hard to remember the names of many of the men I served with, but can easily recall the names of most of the horses.

In addition to the light-hearted foibles I have written about, there are still a few sad, emotional moments included. I have left out the memories of the really terrible incidents that continue to haunt my dreams.

There's an old saying: "Don't look back unless you can smile; don't look ahead unless you can dream."

Garry Leeson

Acknowledgements

I would like to thank all the fellow aspiring authors who, over the years, sat with me and listened to and critiqued my efforts. But most of all I would like to thank my wife, Andrea, for her tireless efforts at dotting my i's, crossing my t's, tossing out the unnecessary and pointing out the currently politically incorrect things I have a tendency to commit to paper.

Garry Leeson

About the author

Garry Leeson is an award-winning author, playwright, auctioneer, and by times, logger and farmer, from the Annapolis Valley in Nova Scotia. His works have appeared in periodicals in Canada and USA; his plays have had productions in Kentville, and Lunenburg and CBC Radio has showcased his short stories.

He was long listed for CBC Writes in the Creative Nonfiction category in 2012, was a recipient of an Arts Nova Scotia grant and, in 2020 received the Margaret and John Savage First Book Award for Non-Fiction for *The Dome Chronicles*.

Garry lives with his wife, Andrea, and a menagerie of animals, in the community of Harmony.

The curious of mind are welcome to visit garryleeson.com.

www.ingramcontent.com/pod-product-compliance
Lightning Source LLC
Chambersburg PA
CBHW061146120626
46546CB00005B/1954